THE ELECTRO STATIC MAN

THE ART OF MILLER HORNS

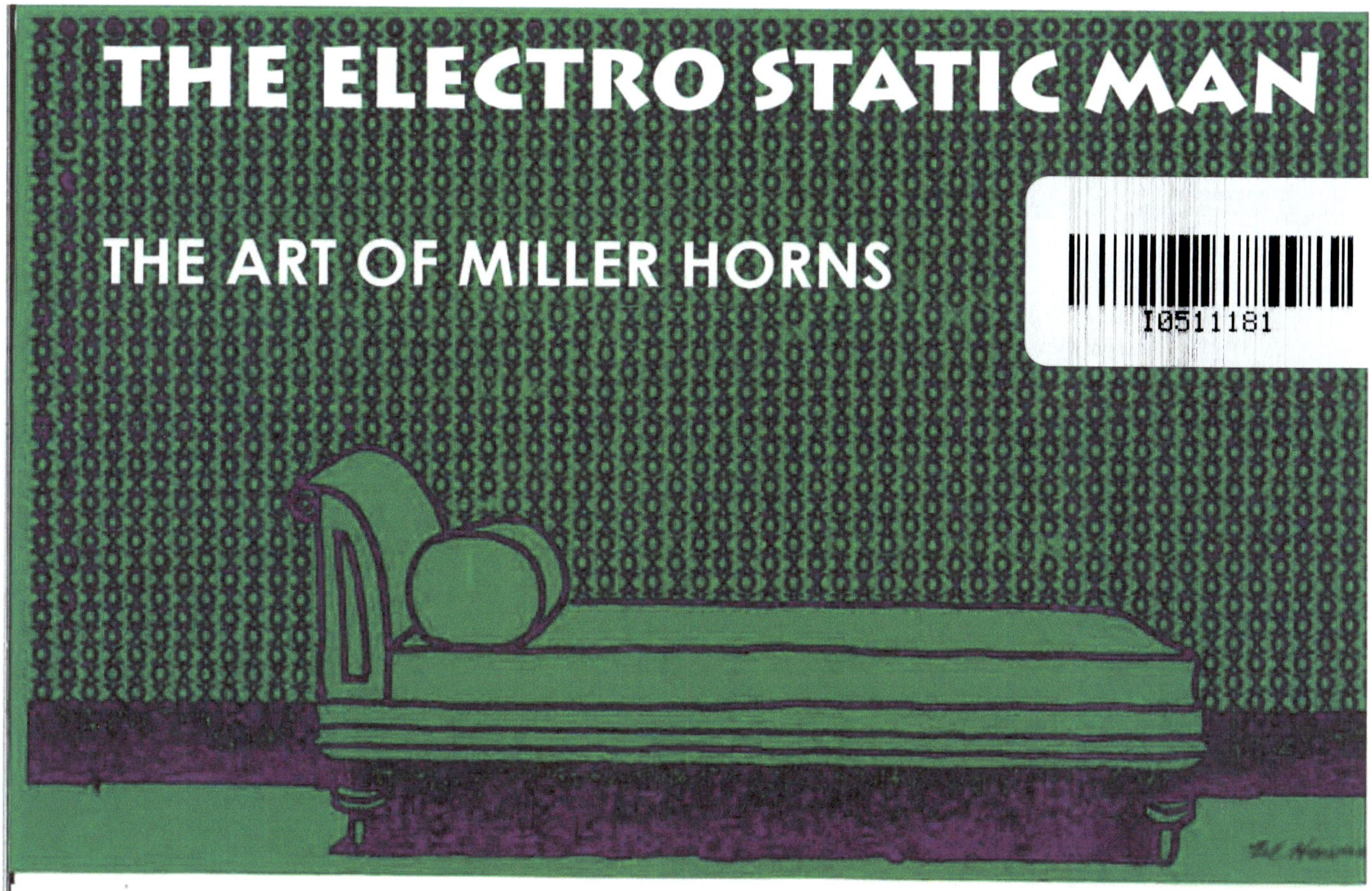

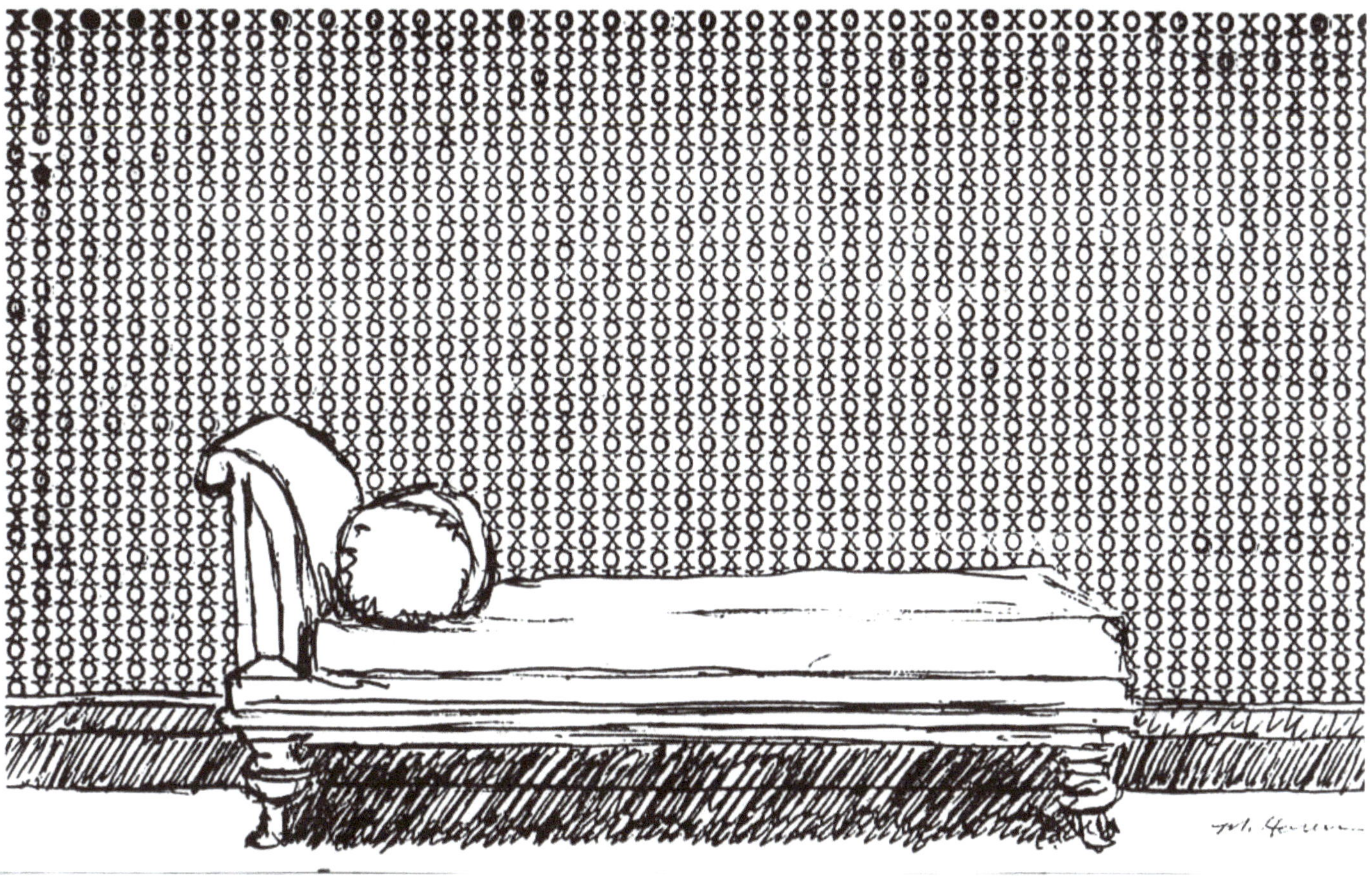

ELECTROSTATIC MAN: THE ART OF MILLER HORNS

Published by: The Artists Archives of the Western Reserve
to accompany the exhibition of the same name

Designed by: Mindy Tousley

Photography of original artwork is courtesy of Bradley Hart or AAWR staff
All depicted works are part of the AAWR collection unless otherwise indicated

THE ELECTRO STATIC MAN

THE ART OF MILLER HORNS (1948 - 2012)

January 27 - March 18. 2017

Presented by
The Artists Archives of the Western Reserve
1834 E 123rd St., Cleveland Ohio 44106

INTRODUCTION

Miller Horns was born in Alabama in 1948. His family moved north, living briefly in Buffalo, NY,and in 1953 to Akron Ohio where he lived out his life. His desire to be an artist might have stemmed in part from undiagnosed dyslexia which caused him to tune out some of his grade school classes and spend his time drawing instead. Drawing and making art became his way of communicating and gaining acceptance and approval from his teachers. He consciously concentrated on art as well as athletics as a way to better himself. He majored in commercial art at The University of Akron, and graduated with a B.F.A. from the Cleveland Institute of Art, in 1986.

By this time he was thoroughly immersed in using the technology of the copy machine to create his works. He described himself in one interview as an "electronic carver". He defined his process in the following way, "The Xerox machine gives what it can and in turn, the artist gives what he can (his talent and abilities) and from this intervention depends the artistic form". Rather than using the copier for simple reproduction his interaction with the machine resulted in changes in texture and, scale. Color manipulation was applied through thermal transfer processes which he learned firsthand from Phyllis Seltzer. Horns loved that the machine allowed him to make large scale works through the often painstaking method of tiling images together. He also liked the fact that he had "broken out of the frame". He produced works that were meant to extend beyond the wall space onto the ceiling and the floor. A feat which would be extremely difficult with a traditional stretched canvas.

Although I have known Miller and his work for some years, as I sifted through the selections for this exhibition and this catalog I was struck by many revelations concerning his practice. First and foremost is the degree of thoughtfulness Horns put into his work. For Miller there was no separation of "Art & Life". He reflected deeply on his personal experiences, his loves, his grief, his life as an African American man, and his struggle as an artist. Every experience was fodder for his art. As Horns described it, "Art is just life. It's what I do in a day. It takes in everything. It's not just my working with a photocopier. And every day is different. It's not repetitious by any means." Absolutely everything in a finished piece by Horns has symbolic meaning, including the frame colors, when the work is framed. He produced works of deliberate art that laid bare universal experiences and emotions so that we could share in them and recognize something of ourselves.

This unique way of making art earned Horns many accolades over the years. In 1989 - 1990 he was selected from 1000 applicants to be a Fellow of the American Academy in Rome. The coveted prize allowed him to live and work in Italy for six months. The Xerox Corporation impressed with his innovative use of their technology, supplied him a machine to use while he was there and the experience overall had a profound effect on his life. Horns was also awarded a residency in 2000 at the prestigious McDowell Colony in New Hampshire, and in 2001 was a guest artist at the historic Yaddo artist community in New York. Horns completed numerous public commissions including murals for the Akron Children's Hospital Medical Center, Advanced Elastomer Systems L.P. and the Maple Valley Branch Library in Akron, Ohio. He wrote and made sets for a dance and play, *Just Passing Through*, which was produced by the Weathervane Theatre and performed by the Firestone High School. He was chosen as Akron's First Night Artist for the 1999 / 2000 millennium celebration, and was also a chosen artist for Guitarmania. Miller devoted the last sixteen years of his life to raising public awareness and support for his design for *The Matthews Hotel Monument* in Akron Ohio. This public monument commemorates the former African-American entertainment district of Howard Street, Akron Ohio. His work has been shown in The Akron Art Museum, The Cleveland Museum of Art, The Museum of Contemporary Art Cleveland, and The Butler Institute of American Art among others.

It was my great privilege to know Miller Horns while he was alive and an even greater privilege to see his work become part of the collection of The Artist Archives of the Western Reserve.

Mindy Tiousley
AAWR Executive Director

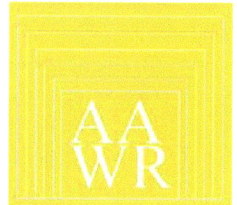

The Artists Archives of the Western Reserve (AAWR) is a unique archival facility and regional museum created to preserve representative bodies of work by Ohio visual artists.

Through ongoing research, exhibition, and educational programs the AAWR actively documents and promotes this cultural heritage for the benefit of the public.

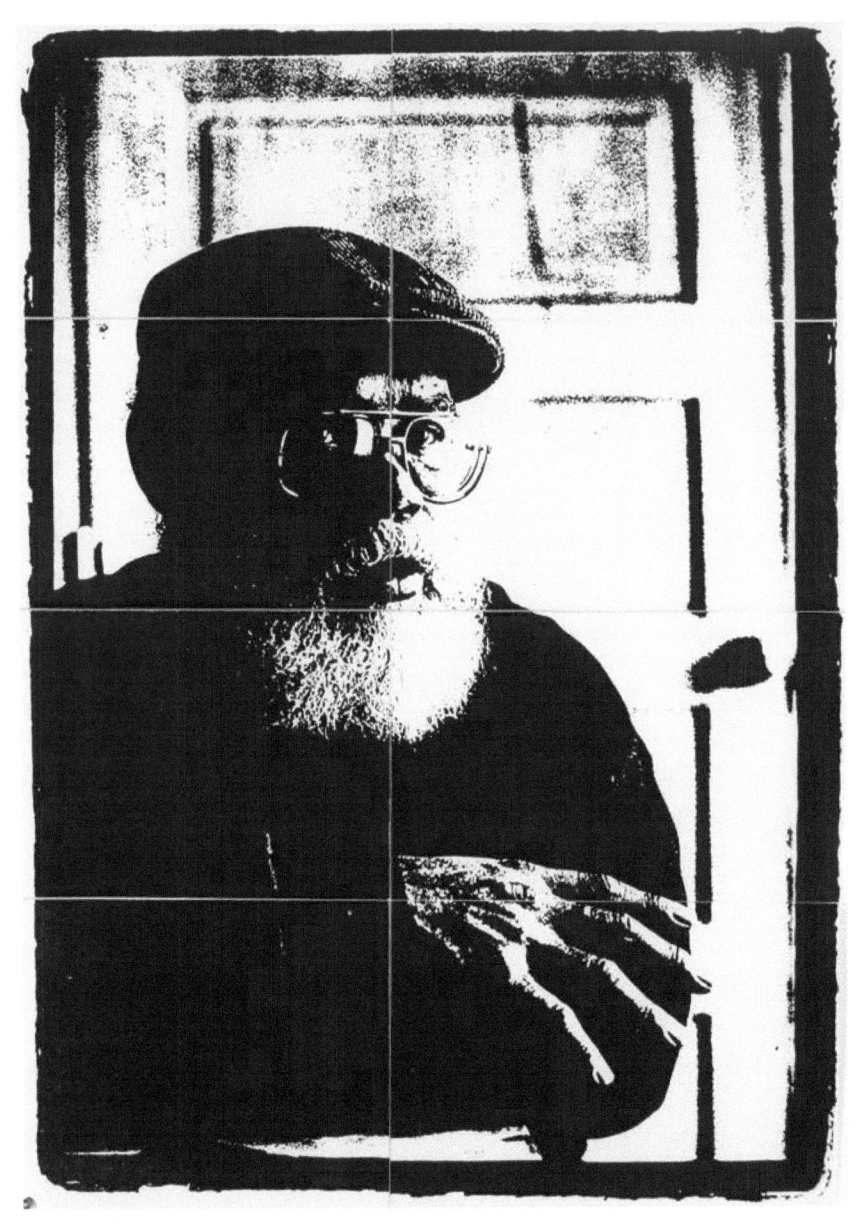

Miller Horns Self Portrait
Electrostatic print, laminated   40" x 27"   circa 2000
photo of original artwork by Bardley Hart

2010 was the year Miller Horns literally walked into my life, or studio as it would be. He was interested in me and my art. I asked him who he was and he proceeded to educate me about himself. He was a soft spoken, articulate man who talked at a careful pace. He was carrying a well-worn satchel that contained documentation of his glowing credentials as an artist. Newspaper articles, magazines, post cards, a resume, and a book. The book was his copy of the "Centennial Directory of the American Academy in Rome". I learned Miller was an AAR Fellow in 1990 in the Design Arts category. I was very impressed, and then things got even more interesting. We were conversing and getting to know each other a bit. He told me about his adventures in Rome and the fun he and AAR Sculpture Fellow David Hammond had while they were there. He asked me who my favorite artist was, and when I told him it was Phillip Pearlstein, Miller replied, "Phillip Pearlstein presented me with my Rome Prize award". I described earlier how impressed I was with Miller? Now it was off the charts!

Miller became a dear friend and mentor to me. Along with his immense artistic talent he was also contemplative, methodical, and persistent. A prime example of a lesson he taught me occurred during a trip together to visit MOCA Cleveland. It was the final show at that location before they moved into their brand new building on Euclid Ave and I wanted to see a particular artist's work. When we arrived I hurriedly walked past a video installation on my way to the exhibit I wanted to see. As usual Miller was walking slowly behind me and called out to me to come back and watch the video. He was very persistent. I said, "OK". It was a video by artist Javier Tellez that was shown at the 2008 Whitney Biennial titled "Letter on the Blind for the use of Those Who See". The video was about six blind people touching a live elephant for the first time, capturing their moments of tactile recognition. It was so powerful to me and still is to this day. Because of Miller I no longer quickly dismiss work that is out of my comfort zone.

Miller taught me a lot about persistence. He spent the last years of his life working to get his *Mathews Hotel Monument* built in Akron. It was to be built on land designated as a State Historical Landmark. Miller was the person responsible for getting this designation for the site. From the time Miller came up with the original concept and proposal, convinced the city government of its importance, and acquired the support from the public and donors, until the time it was built, took sixteen years. At this point Miller's health had begun to fail, but he did live long enough to see the monument completed before he passed away. At Millers memorial service Akron Deputy Mayor Dave Liebert spoke affectionately about Millers persistence in seeing that the project was finished. It now stands as a physical testament to the man I call "the single most positive male influence in my entire life".

Thank you, Miller.

Terry Klausman 2016

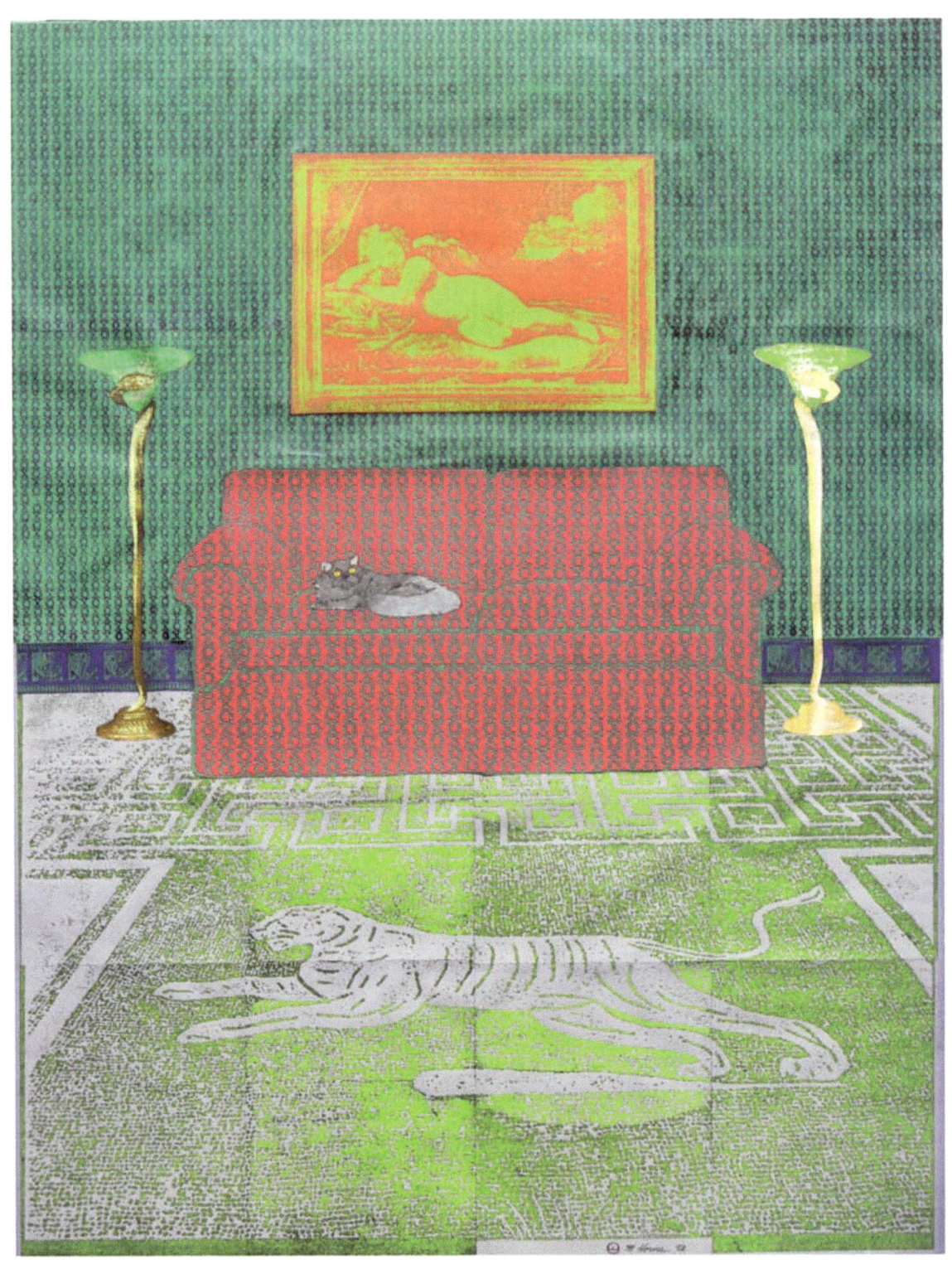

X's Libido   electrostatic and thermal transfer print collage   34" x 23"   1992

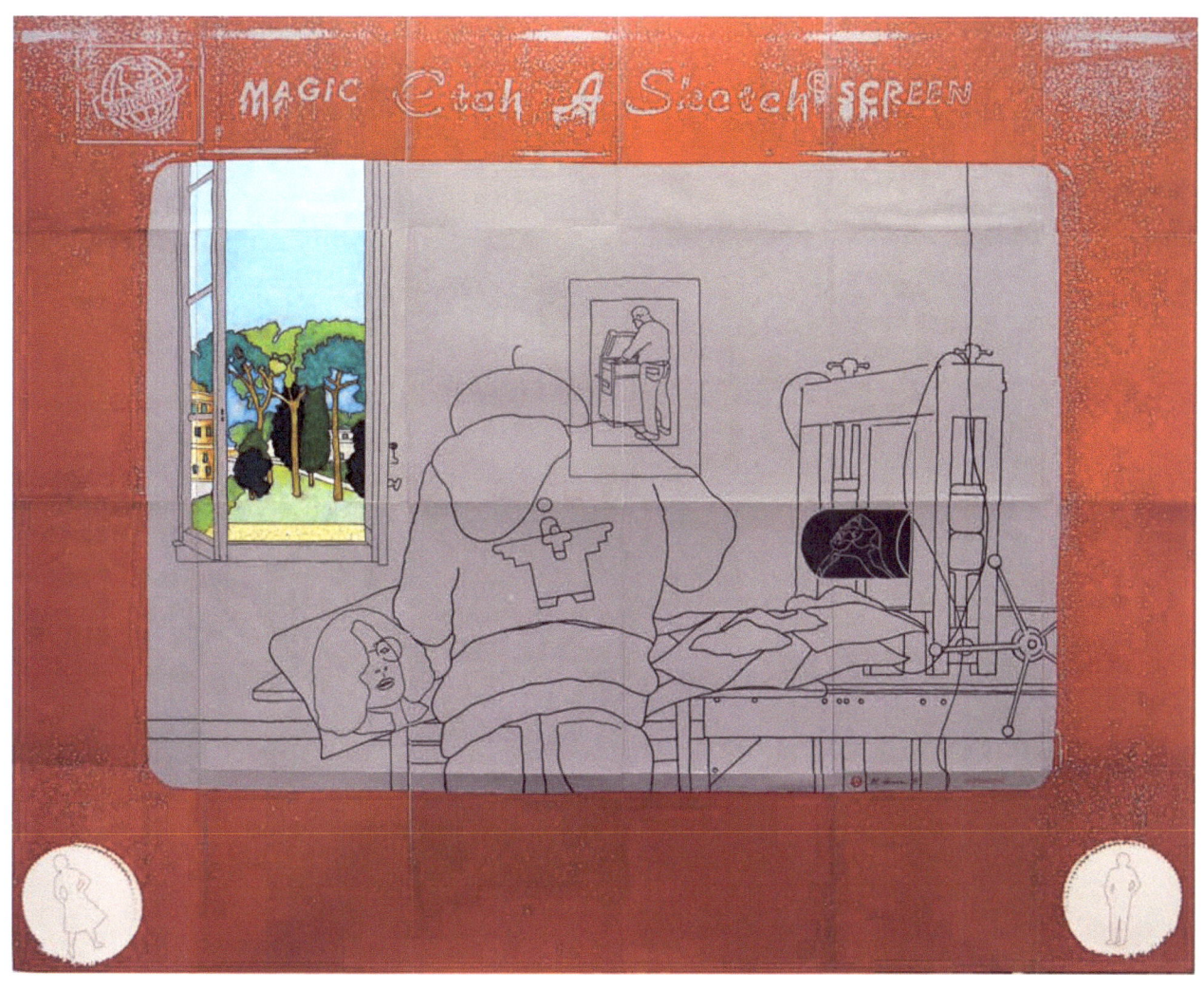

Pulling of the Proof   electrostatic print collage   37" x 44"   1991

This is a portrait of two artists working side by side, Miller Horns and Rosemary Marino. Rosemary is a traditional print maker while Miller is shown using a copy machine. The Etch - A - Sketch is symbolic of the playfulness of childhood. The out door scene, the artists ability to create a fresh world. The gray color represents seriousness while working, and the inclusion of two artists, one male and one female represent the duality of the relationship and the singularity of their purpose, the creation of Art.

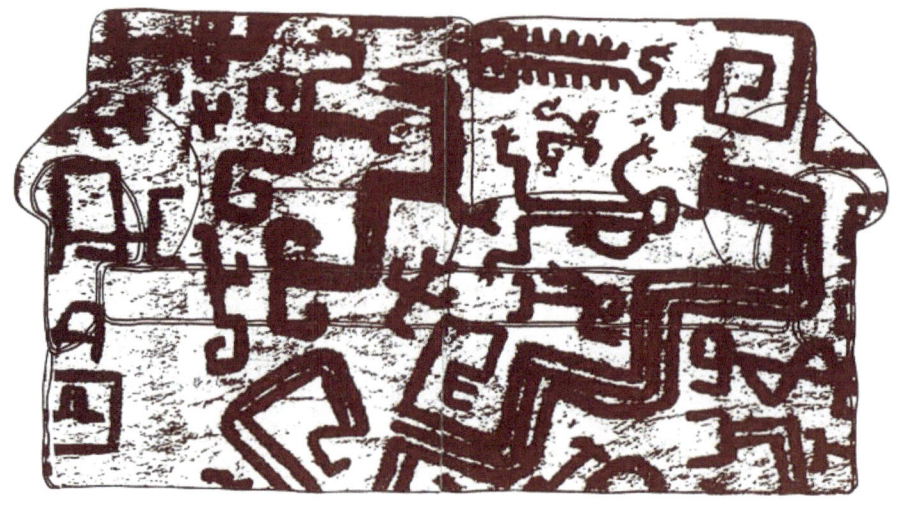

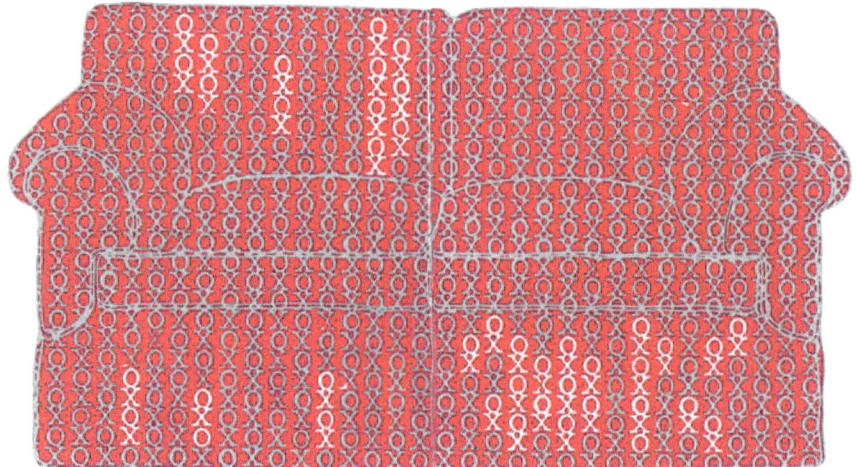

These six 4" x 9"
electrostatic and
thermal transfer
prints are examples
of the types of
multiples that
Miller would make
to use in his work.

He would methodically
try many different
combinations before
a work was finalized.

All of the X's and O's
seen in these small
chairs and in the
X's Libido work
were typed on a
typewriter before
being copied for
use.

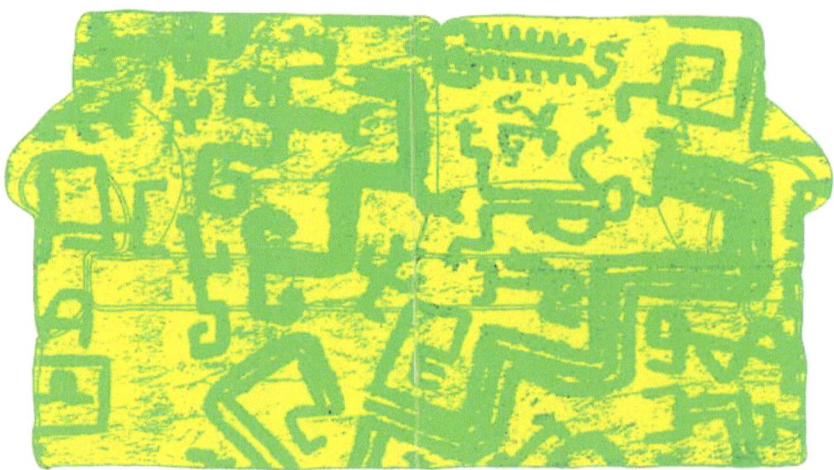

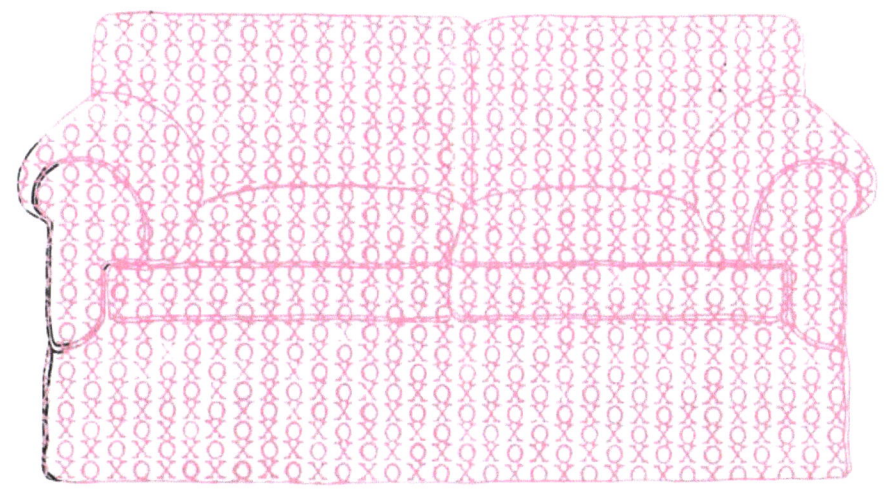

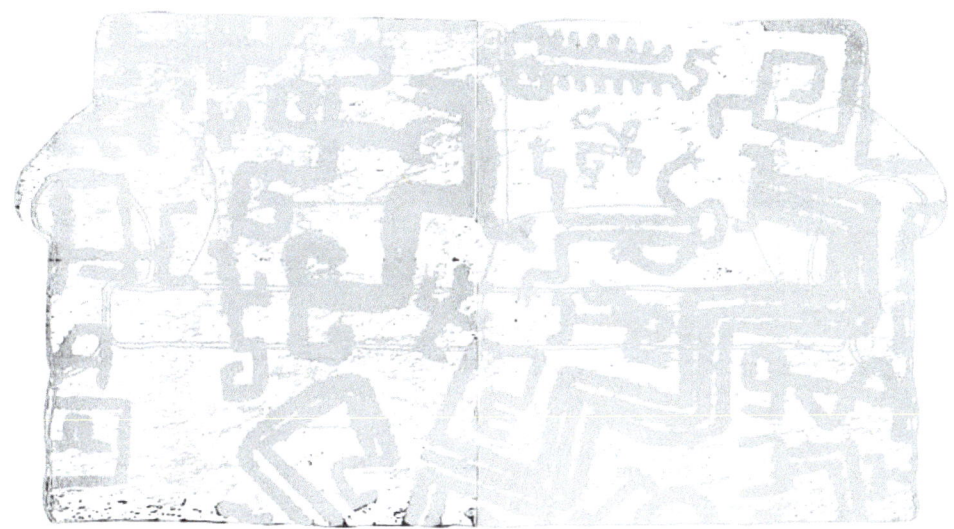

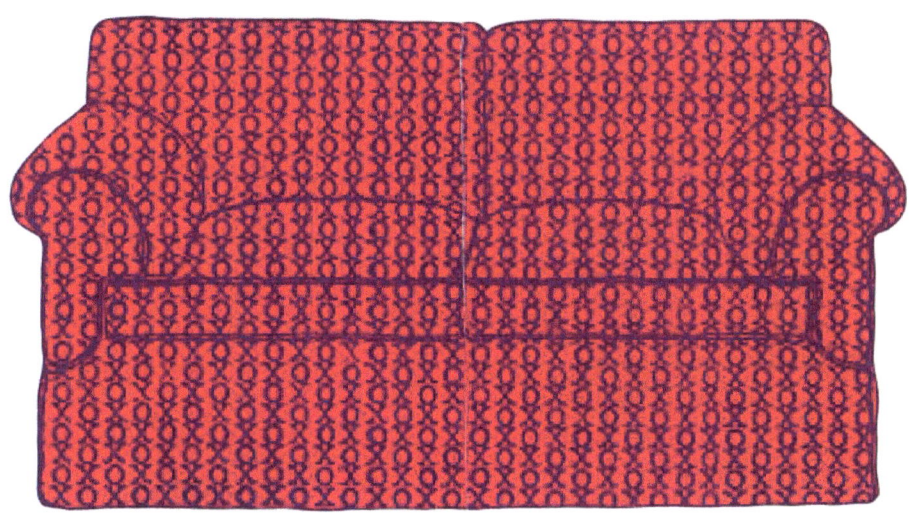

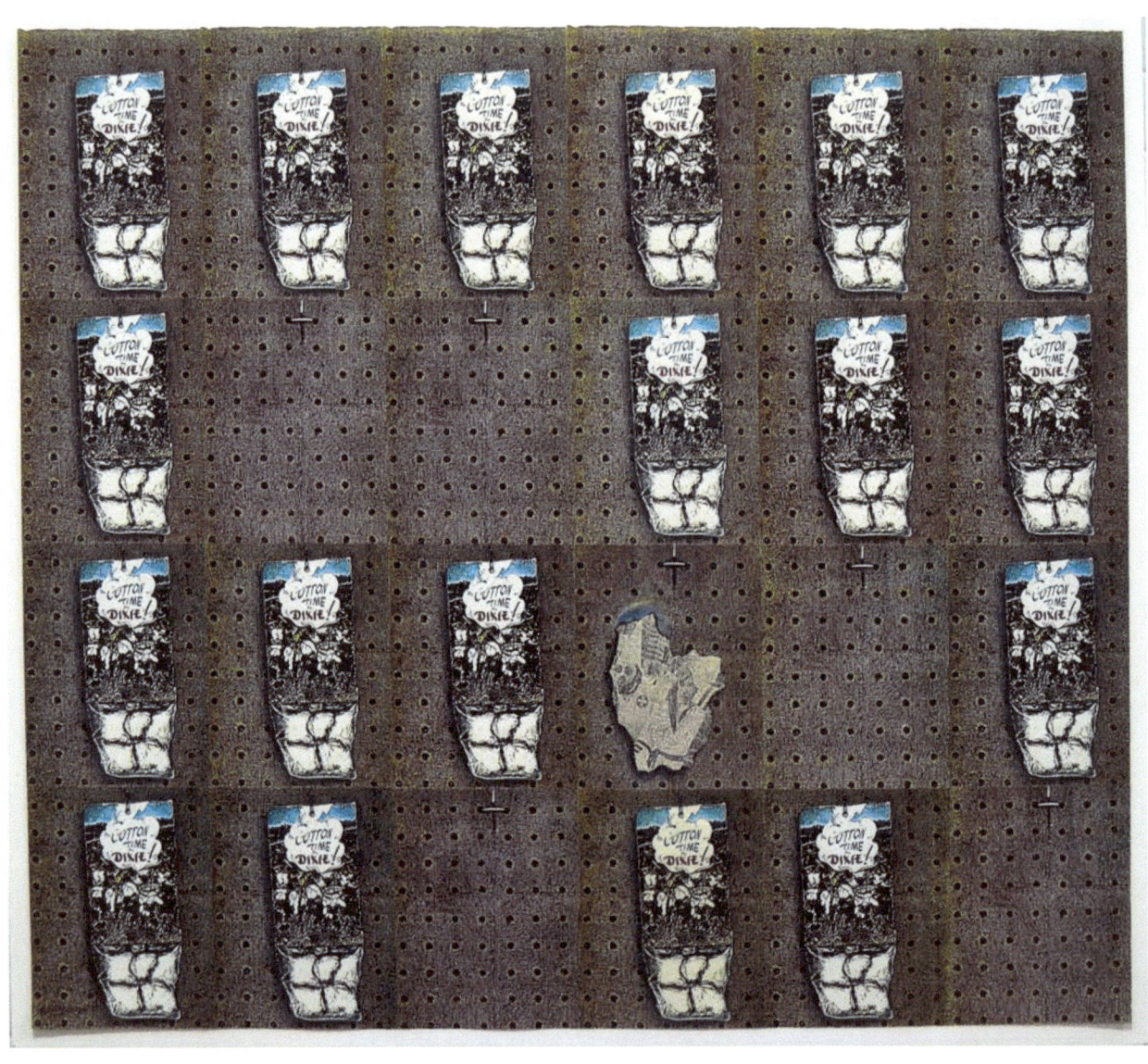

Cotton Time in Dixie   electrostatic print on paper   23" x 20.5"   circa 1982

Untitled
electrostatic print
on paper
72" x 32"
1997

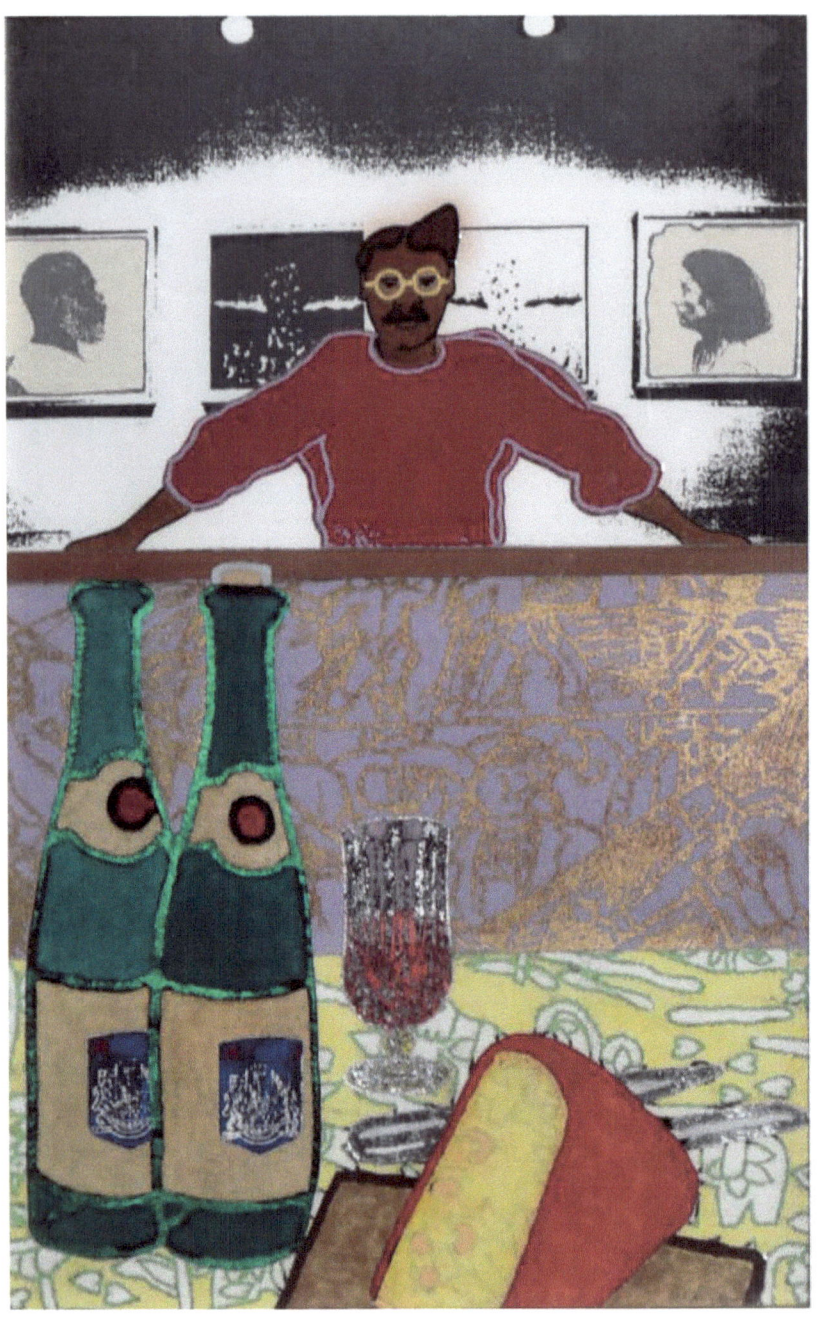

Calvary (one version) colorized print on paper   14.5" x 10"   1992

The title of this work refers to Horns reflections on the vulnerability
of an artist when he exhibits work to the public. He likens the experience
where the art is literally pinned to the wall and artist is subjected to
criticism to being crucified. He also compares the honor of being
exhibited and the sacrificial wine and cheese offered to participants
at the opening reception to the religious experience of communion.

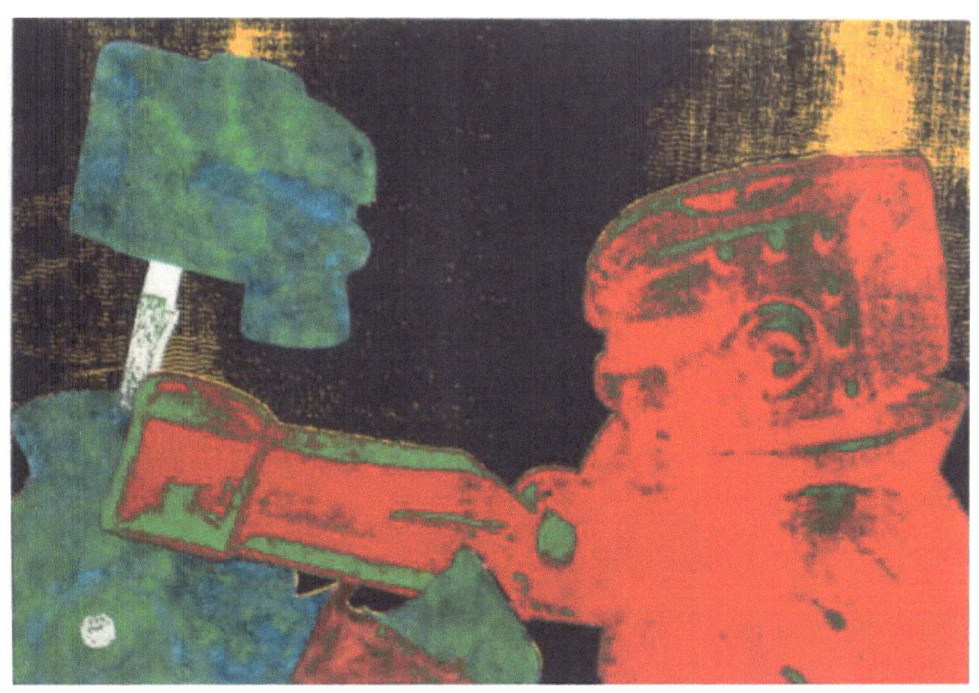

Untitled (Rock 'em Sock 'em Robots)   electrostatic print on paper
7.5" x 10"   1990

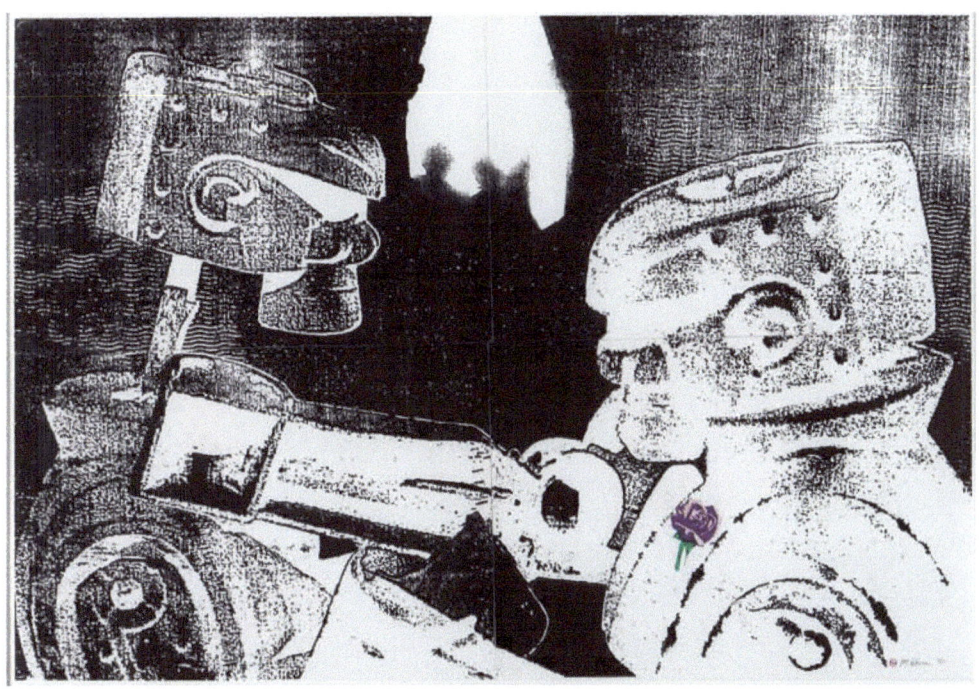

Toyen with Rose   electrostatic print on paper   21" x 30"   1990
Private Collection   Photography of original artwork by Bradley Hart

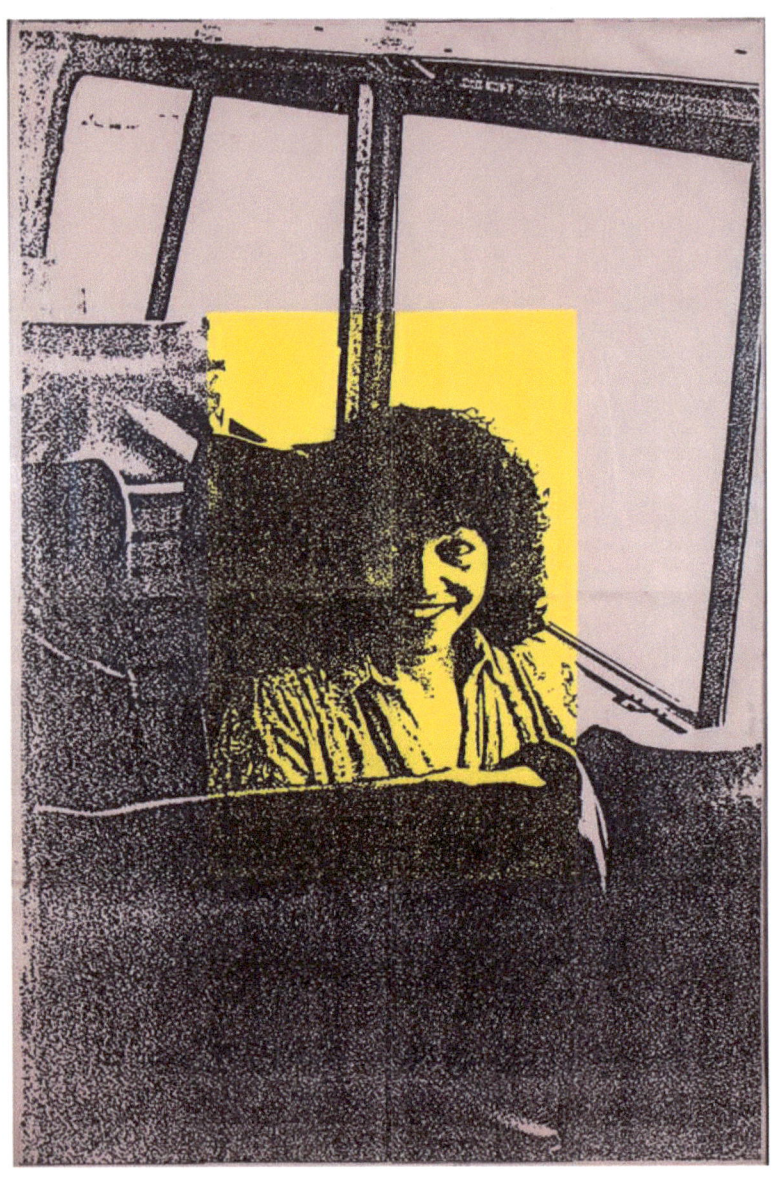

Untitled (Cindy Washington)   electrostatic and thermal transfer
print on paper   40.5" x 27.5"   1984

Photography of original artwork by Bradley Hart

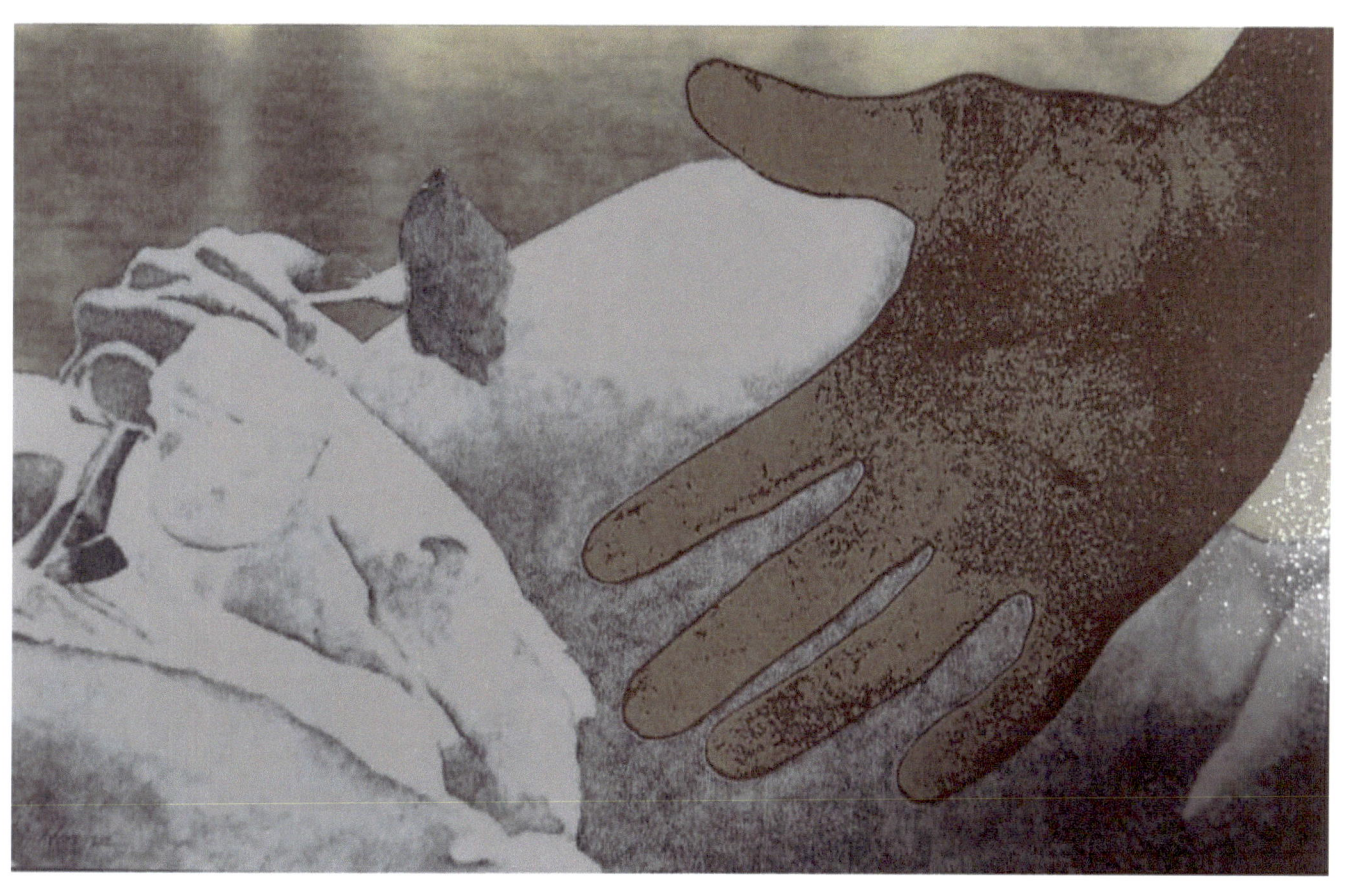

Untitled   electrostatic and thermal transfer print on paper, laminated   12" x 15"   date unknown

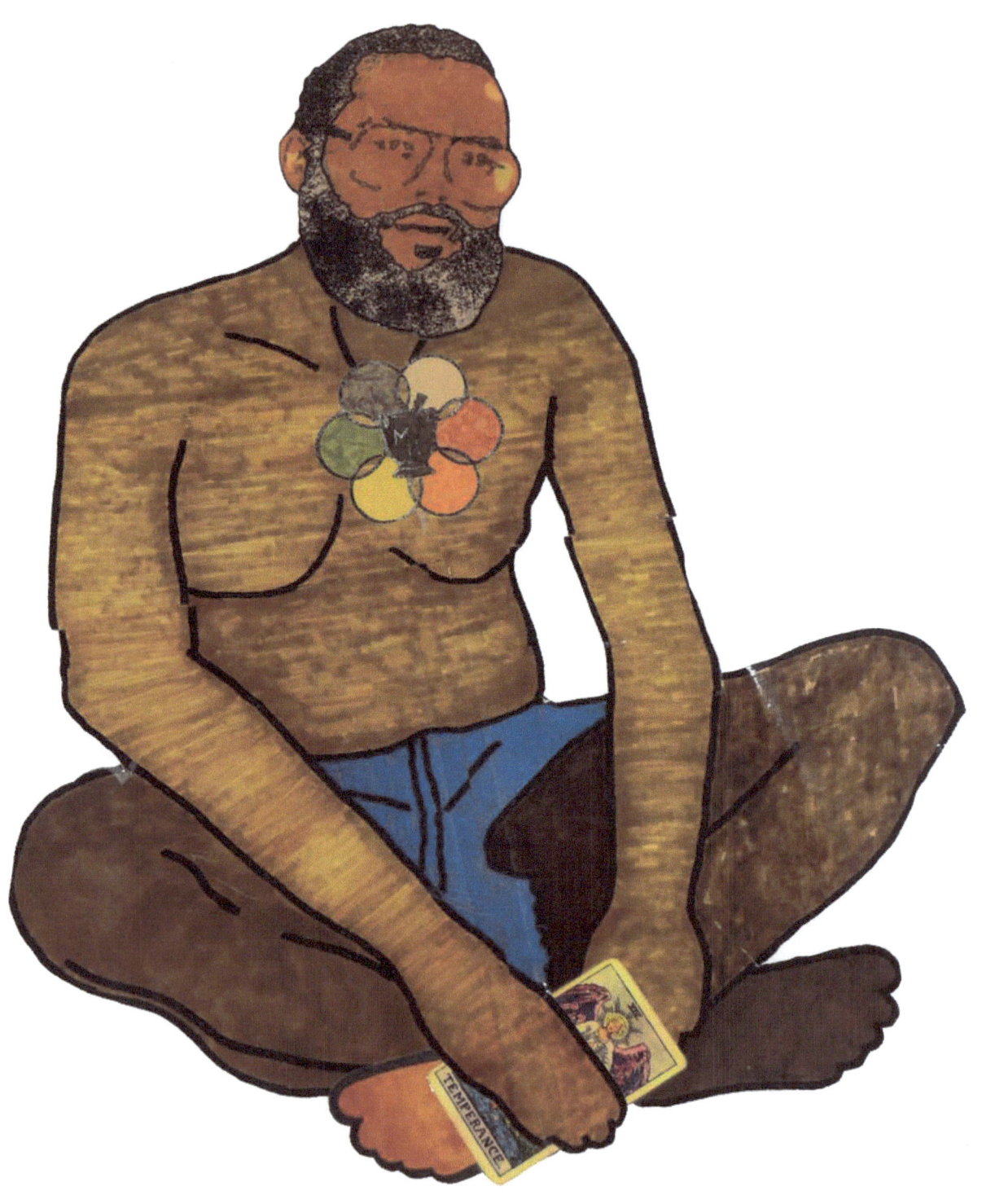

Untitled (Self Portrait)   electrostatic print with marker laminated   28" x 28"
date unknown

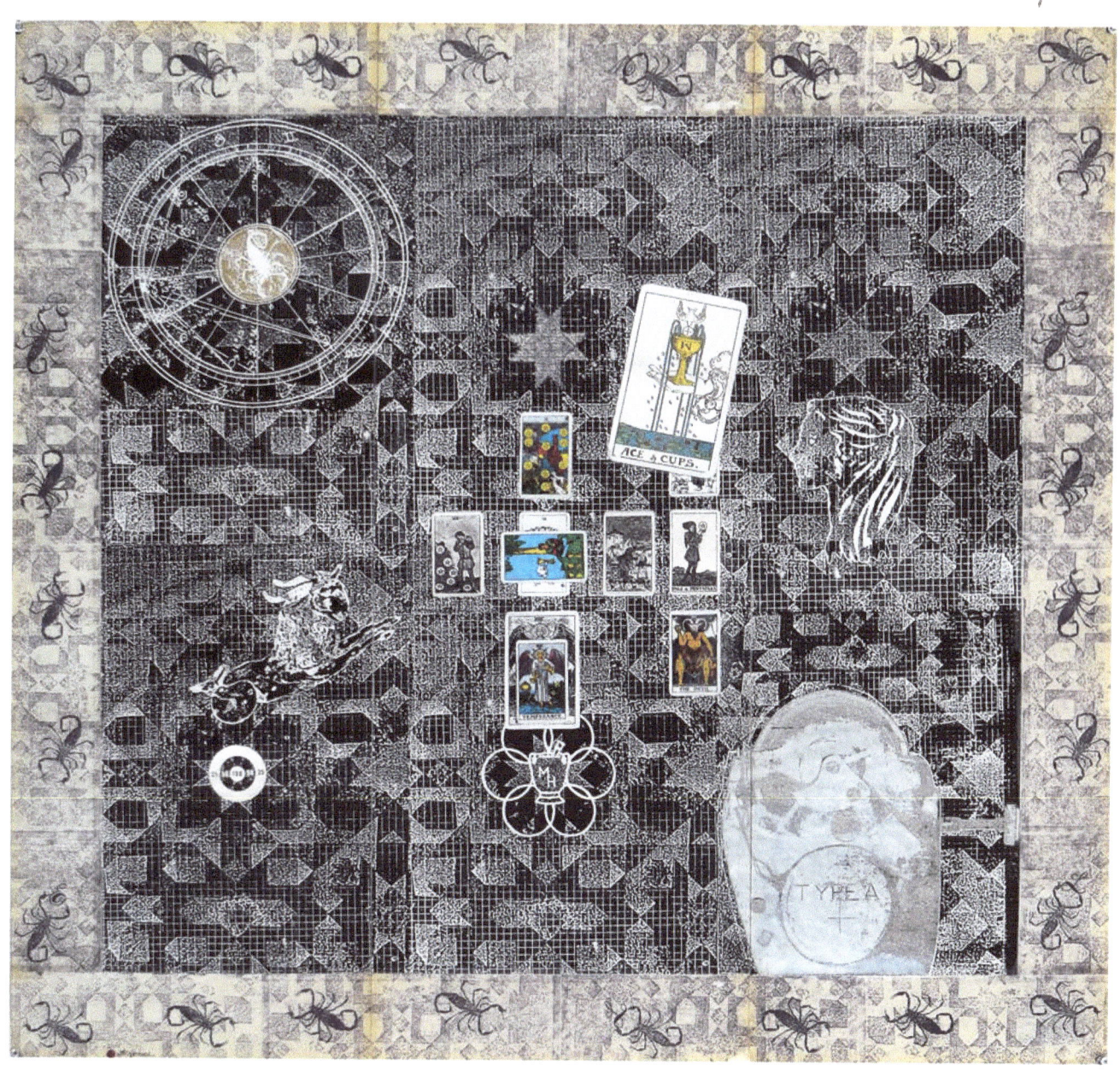

Untitled   electrostatic print laminated   38.5" x 39.25"   date unknown

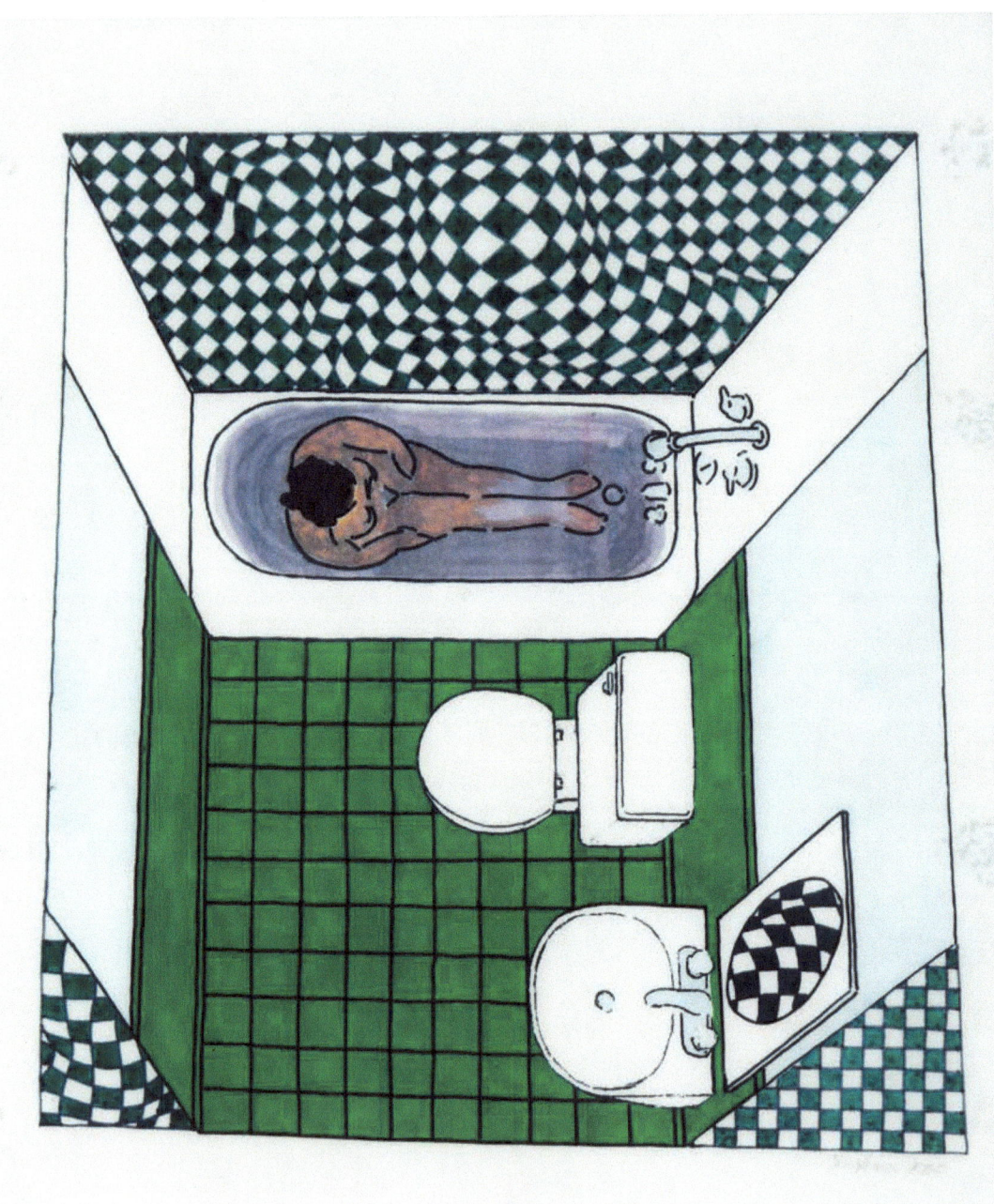

Opt Out Artist   electrostatic print and applied color on paper,
laminated   10" x 9.5"   2000

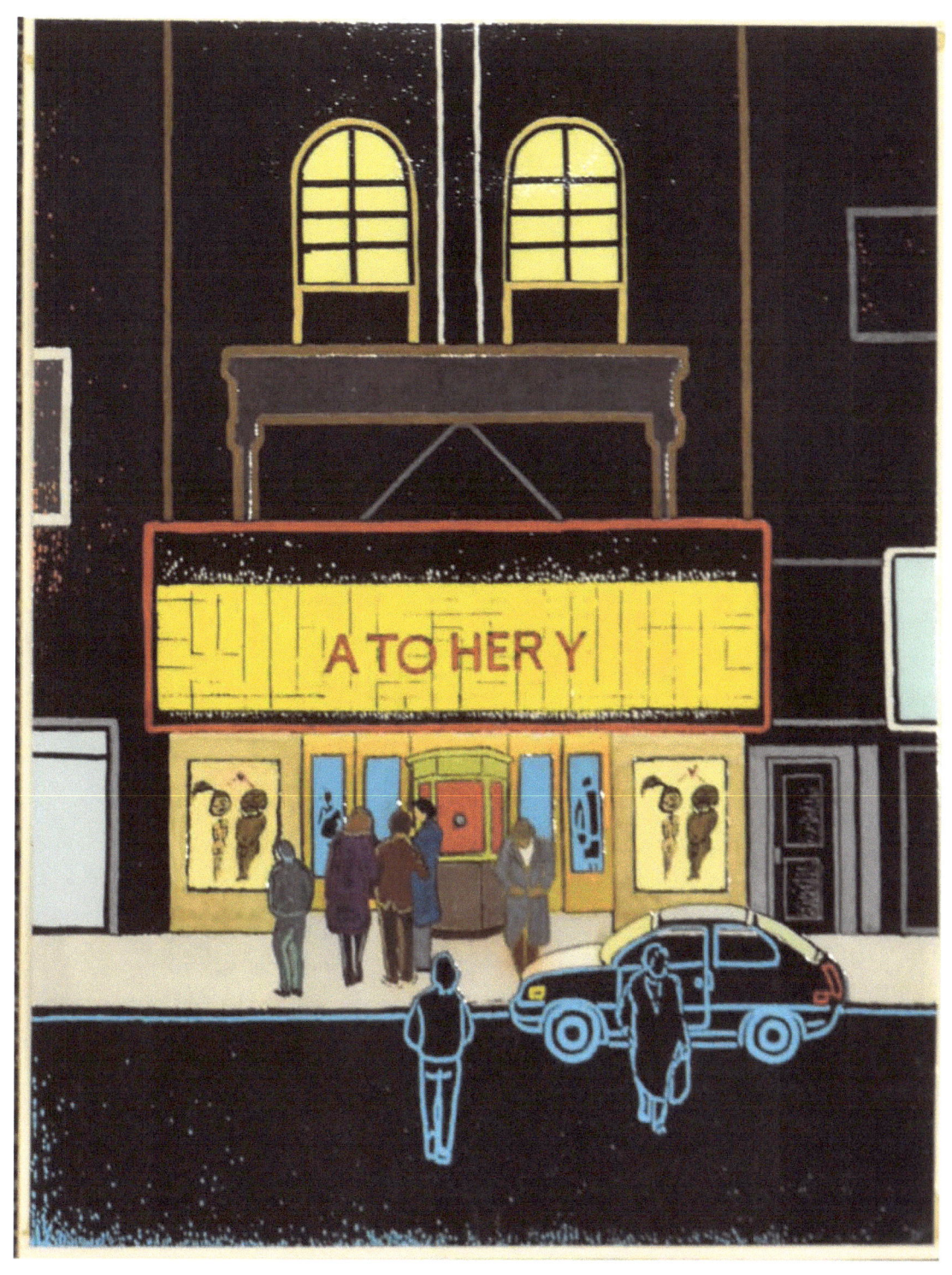

Class Act   electrostatic print, with thermal color transfer on paper
14.5" x 10"   1992

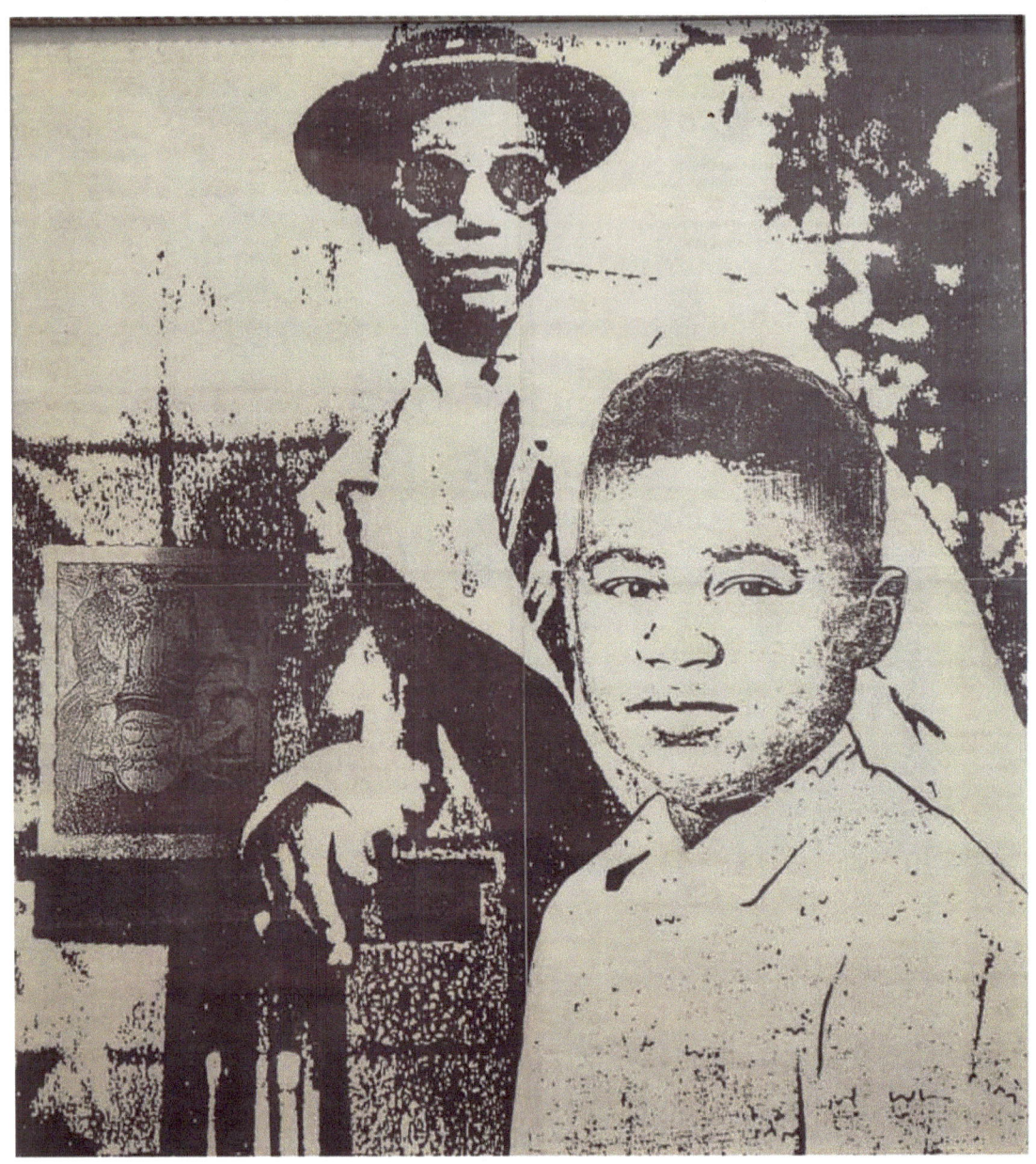

Closure electrostatic print on paper 40" x 27"

This is a double self portrait of Horns as a boy and as a man and as a Rome Prize winner (background *Roma, Rome*). Miller did not know his father and the image of his father in between the two self portraits in this work is from the only photograph he had of him. Making this work was cathartic for him in regards to that relationship and came about after the death of his mother in 1994.

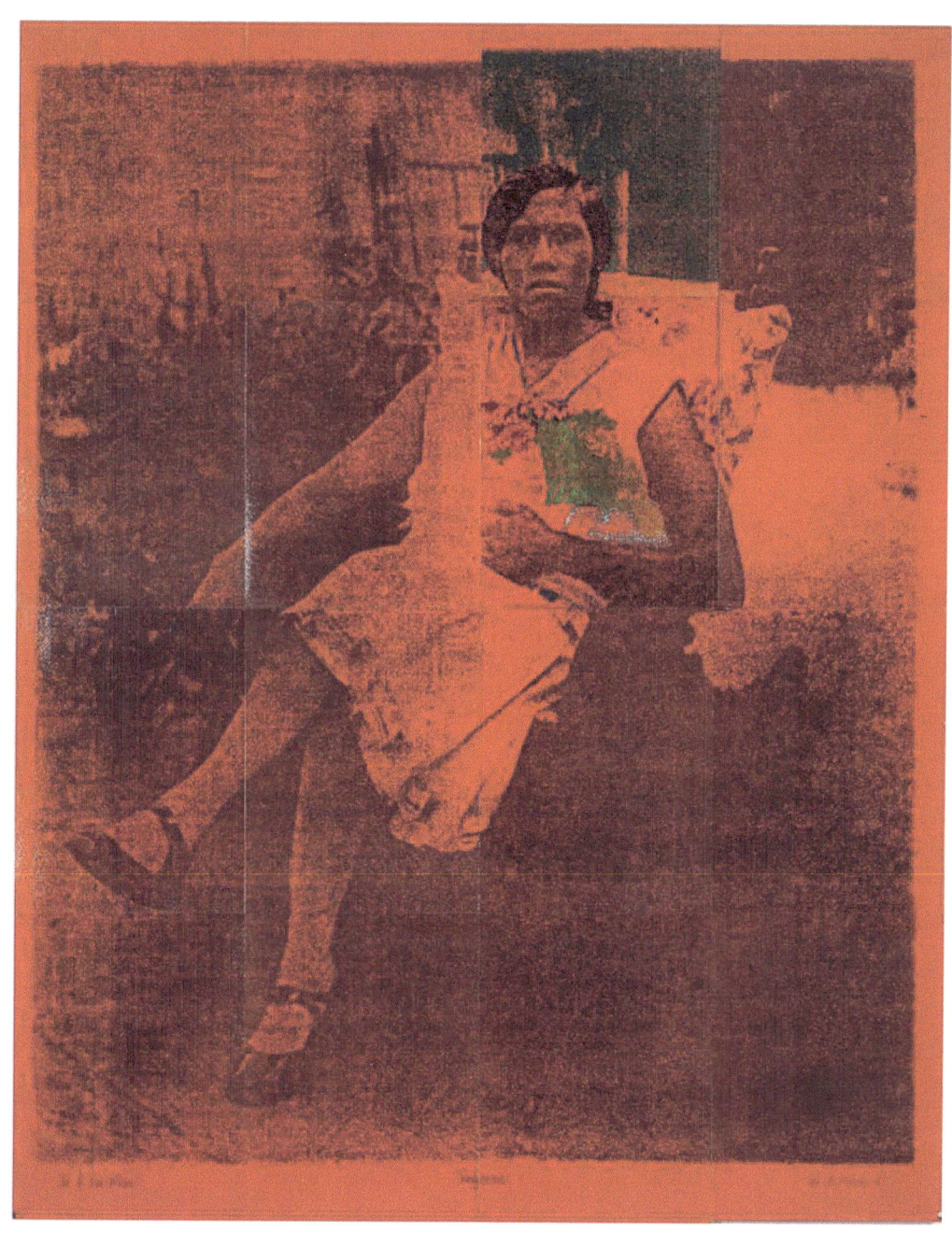

To and for Mom (Tangerine)   42" x 32"   electrostatic print and thermal color transfer on paper laminated   1987

Photography of original artwork by Bradley Hart

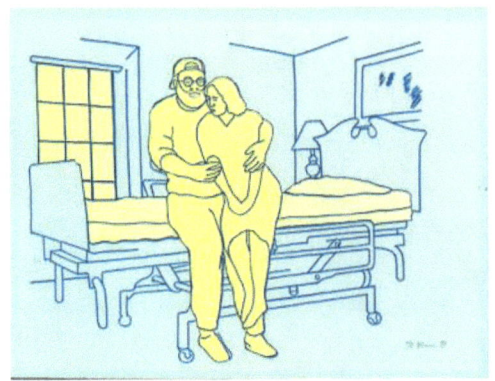

Mother & Son (Don't Have), a series
of 4 electrostatic, thermal color
transfer, and laminated prints
each is 8" x 10" 1995

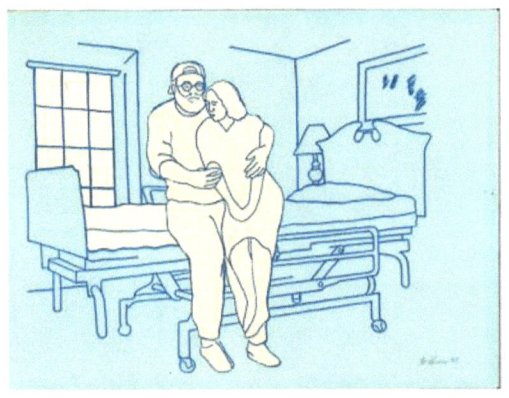

Horns and his mother enjoyed a close
relationship. Following her death in 1994
he went through a period of inconsolable
grief which caused him to reconcile his
past and then document it with images of
hope.
The images on the facing page,
Butch, Am I Losing Weight?, were
based on the beginning of his mothers
illness. As her cancer progressed she was
moved into a hospice facility, which
inspired the *Mother & Son* images on the
left. In the first three Horns is depicted
with his mother and as the series
progresses the color fades out. Note in the
third image both figures now have their
eyes open, so that they can face her
coming death.

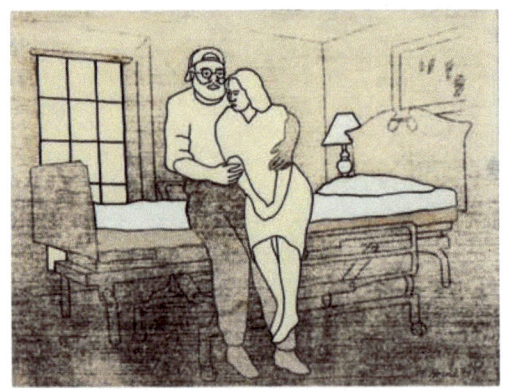

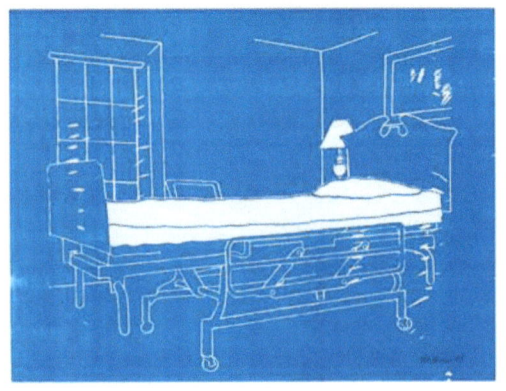

Facing page:

Butch, Am I Losing Weight ?
2 electrostatic, thermal color
transfer, and laminated prints
each is 14" x 11" 1995

Grief Bed
Electrostatic print on paper, laminated
24" x 30" circa 1995

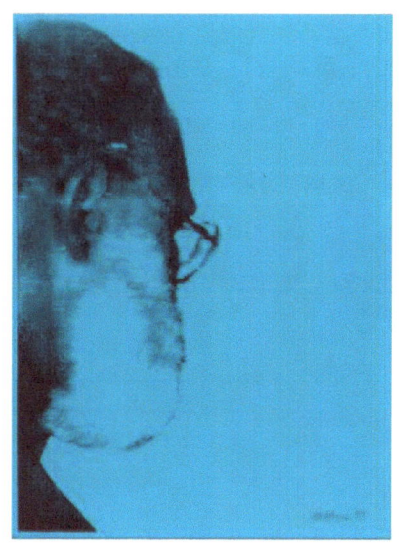
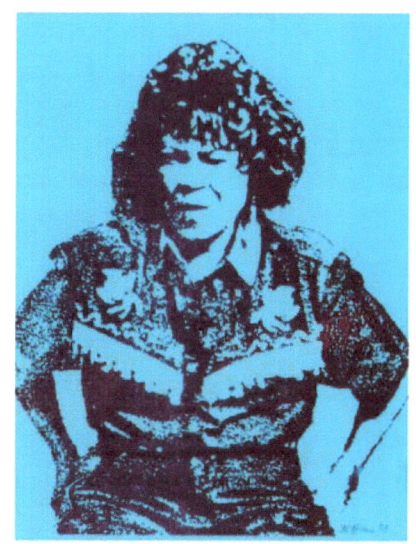
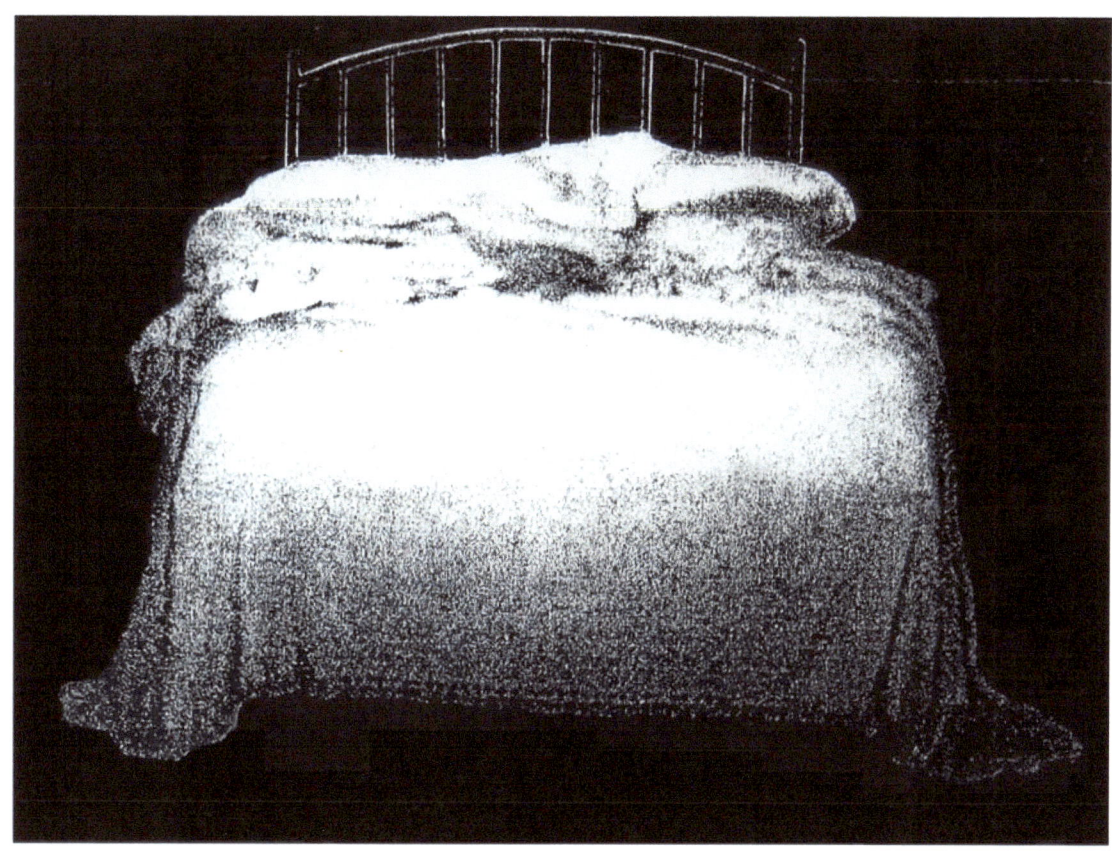

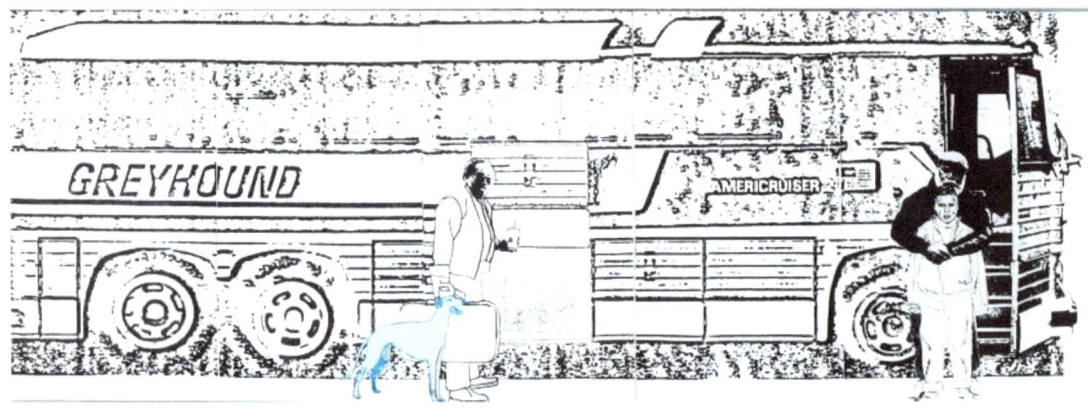

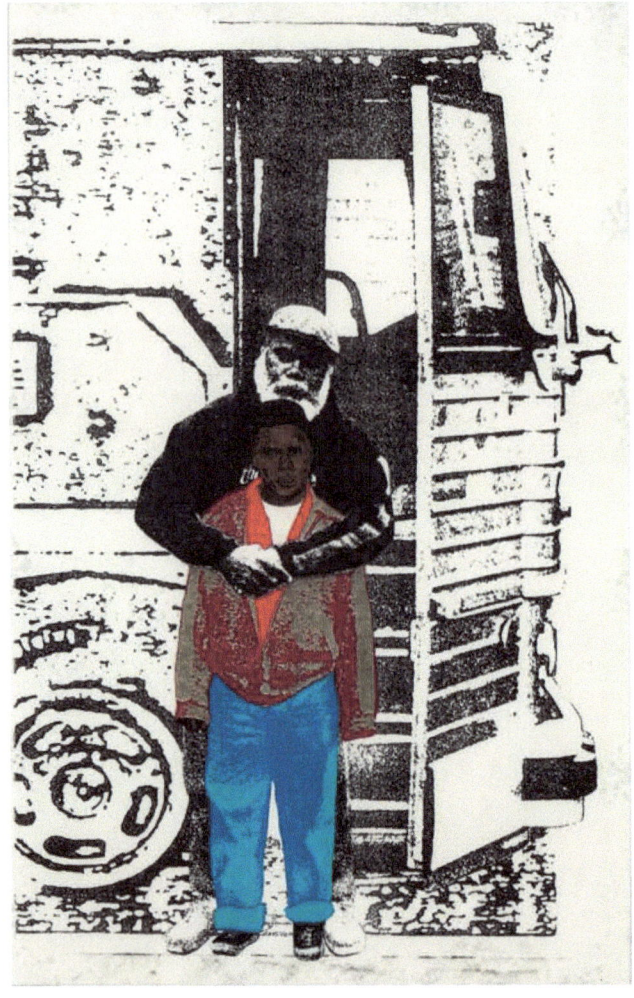

Reunion   electrostatic print on paper
6.5" x 10.75"   1995

The death of Horn's mother put an end to an ongoing series of works, revolving around the Greyhound bus. He started using the bus as symbolic imagery to represent himself moving through life looking for a safe harbor. *Just Passing Through,* (above) both a monumental work on paper measuring 9' x 25', and also a play written by Miller, represents Horn's journey through life. The smaller work on this page, *Reunion*, is included in the larger work and shows a double self portrait of an older Miller embracing his younger self. In the larger work the driver is also shown by the side of the bus, with the luggage door open. "You have to go within yourself," Horns said. "With my mother's death, that's when the bus stopped and that's when I opened up the side of the bus and got rid of that baggage."

Just Passing Through   electrostatic print on paper   8' x 25'   1990
where abouts unknown

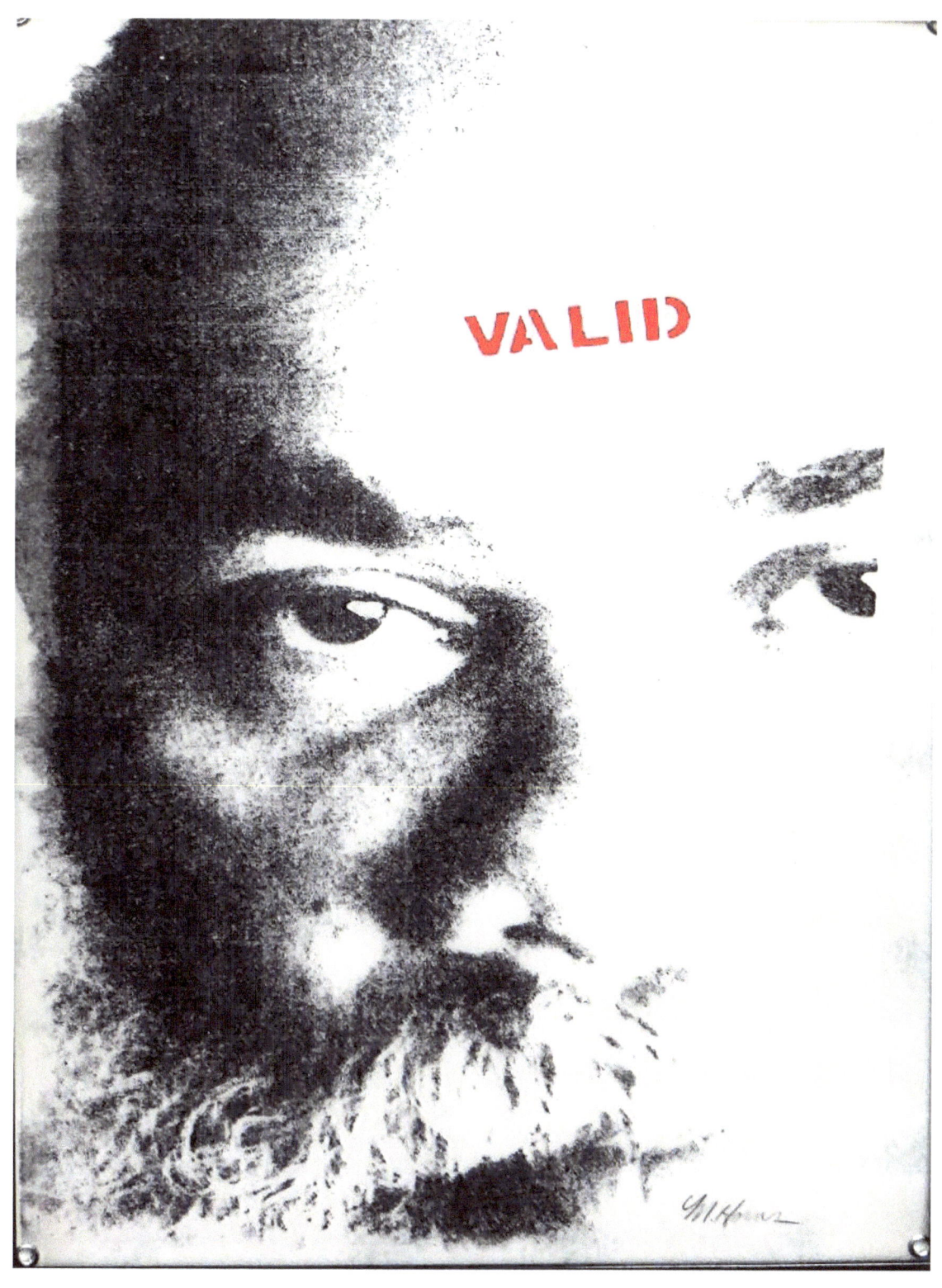

Valid   electrostatic print on paper   17" x 11"   2006
Photography of original artwork by Bradley Hart

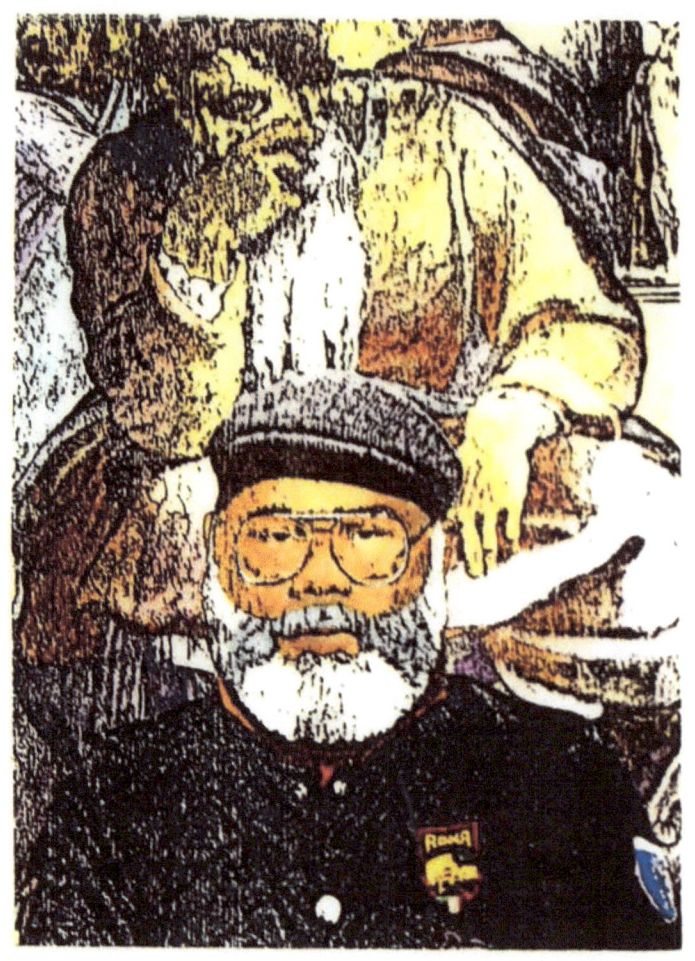

Roma, Rome   electrostatic print on paper laminated   4.5" x 3"
1990

While Horns was in Rome as an NEA/AAR Fellow in Advanced Design,
he visited the Sistine Chapel which was undergoing restoration. He got
to climb the scaffolding to view the ceiling up close but was not allowed
to photograph the ceiling. He then purchased a post card with the image
you see here on it, superimposed his self portrait on top of that and
manipulated it using a machine supplied to him by the Xerox Corporation
to create this work of art. A version of this remains on permanent display
as part of the American Academy of Rome's collection.

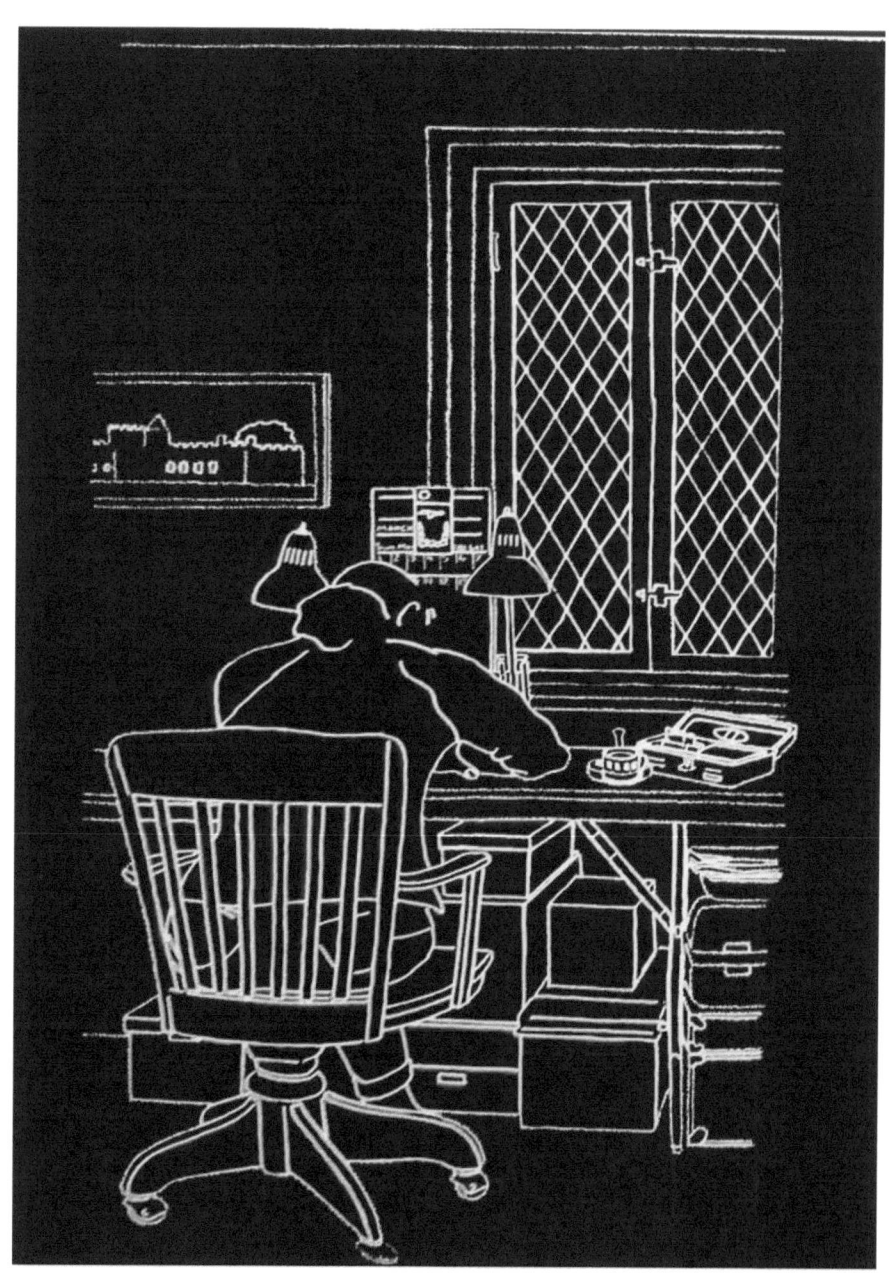

Untitled electrostatic print on paper laminated 46" x 37.5"
date unknown The windows identify this as a depiction of Miller at his desk in Rome, Italy.

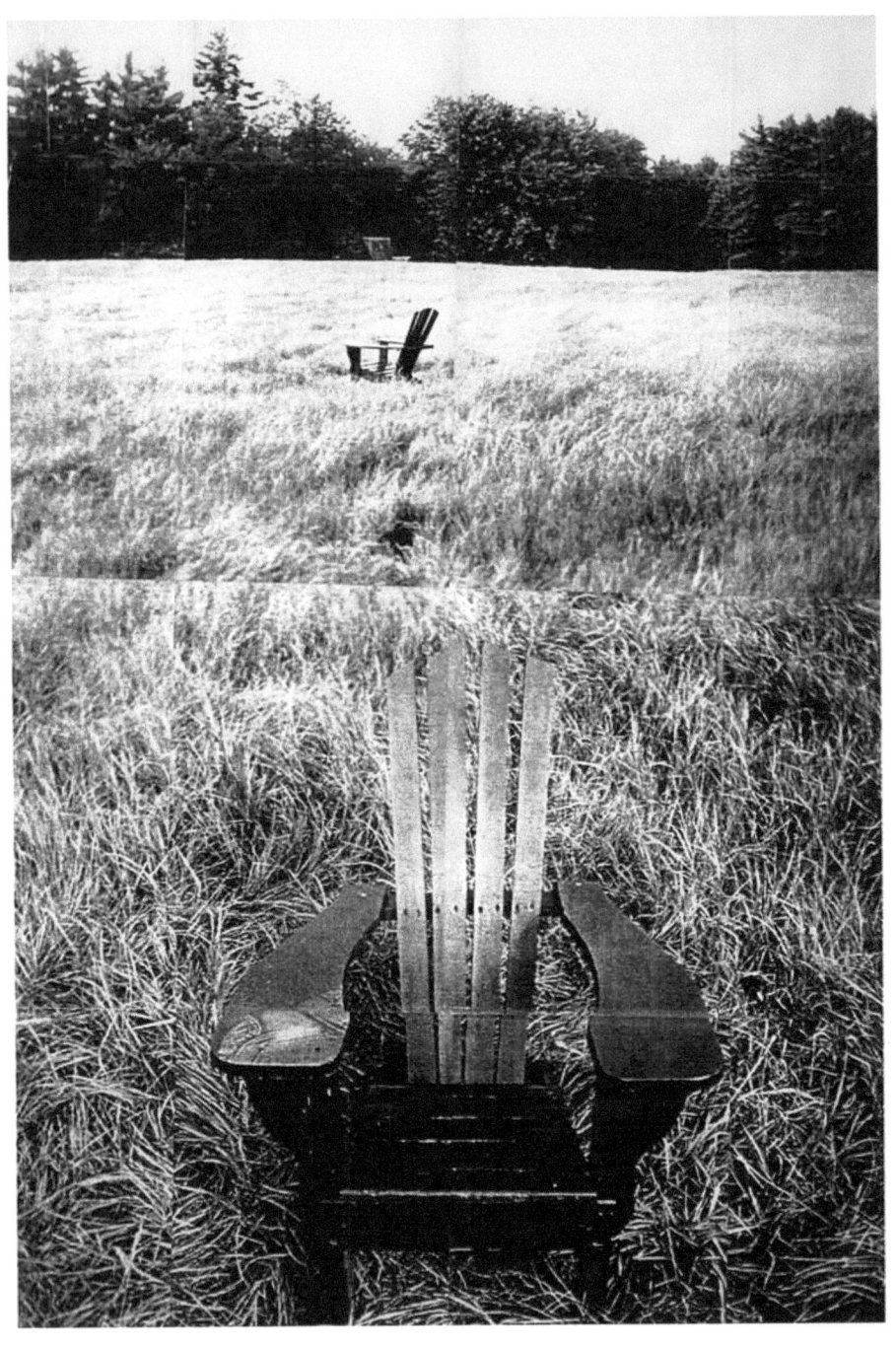

Space, Rest and Atmosphere   electrostatic print on paper, laminated
38" x 28"   2000

Timber
electrostatic print on
paper, laminated
74.5" x 17"
2000

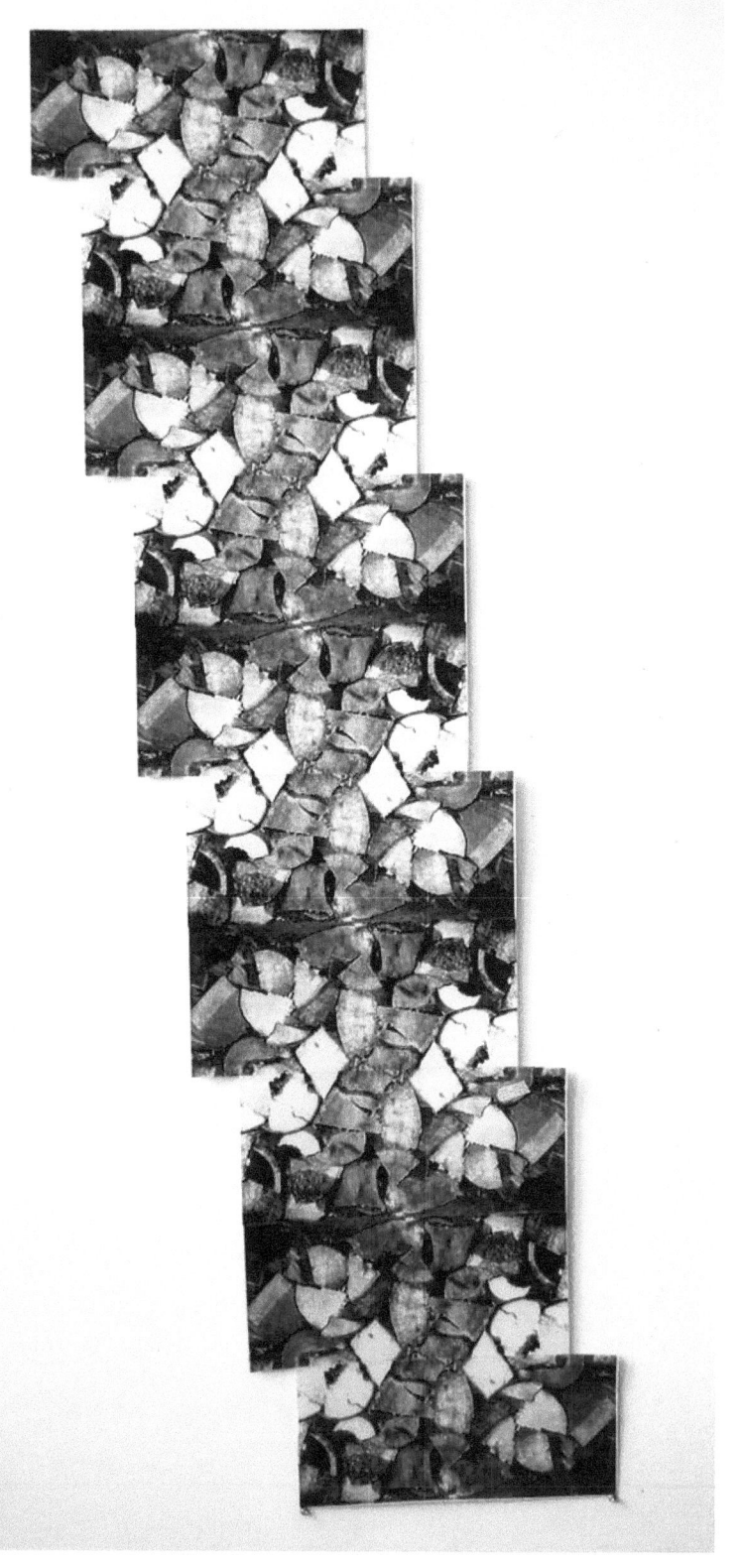

The work on these pages is
part of a series of works
completed during Horns residency
at the prestigious McDowell Art
Colony in New Hampshire.
The work is simpler and based
on his direct experiences of
nature and his everyday
life while at McDowell. The
obvious self referentialism that
characterized his past work is
now hidden or implied in these
new pieces. The empty chairs in
Space, Rest and Atmosphere or
the shadow of himself in, *I Love
My Bicicletta.*
He wrote of this work, "In the
past I've alternated between
the black and white, but now
with elemental subjects like
blades of grass, leaves and
water, I prefer the black and
white because it allows me
to highlight both the surface
texture and underlying
structure of things. '

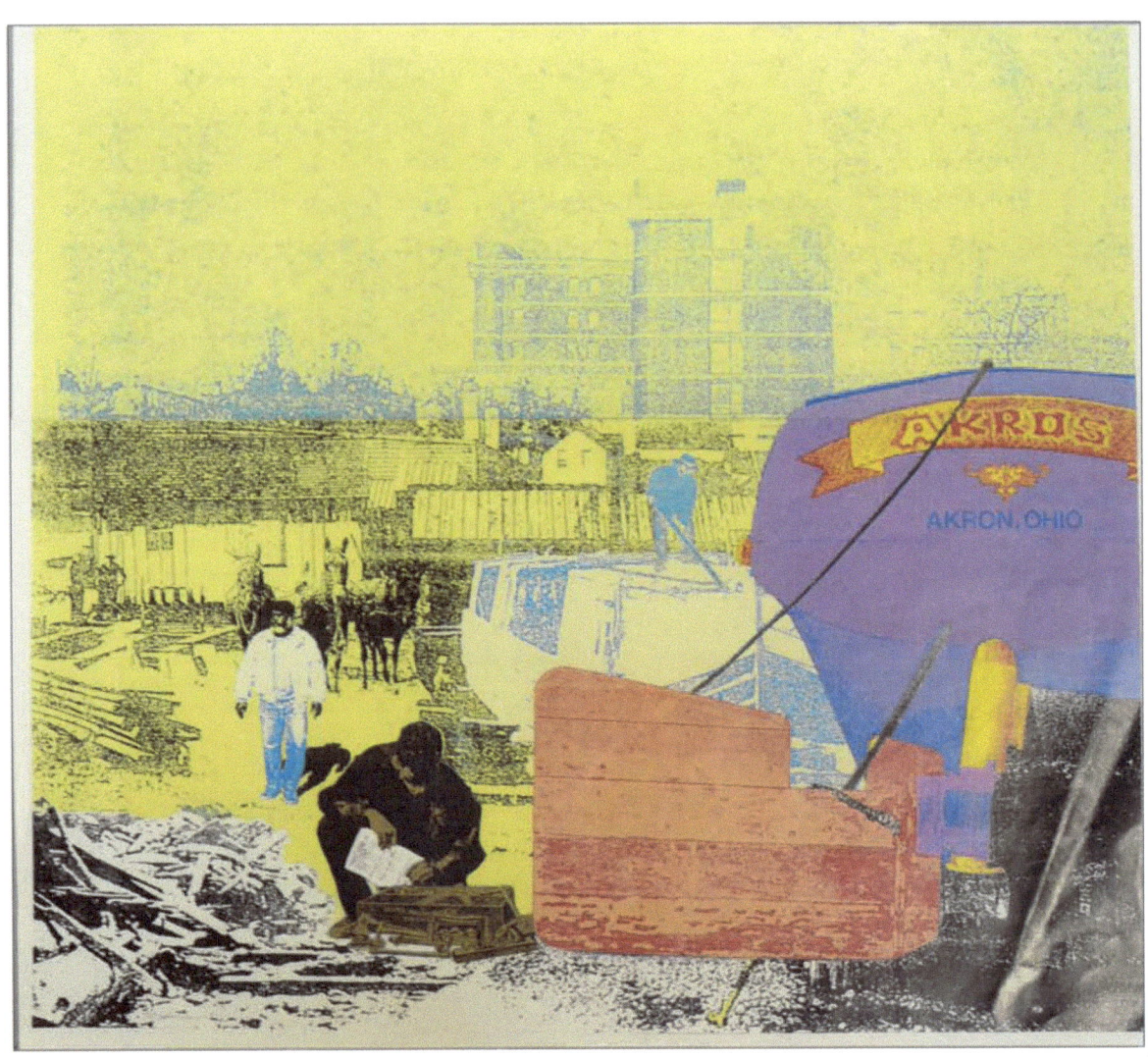

Akros: Lock 2   electrostatic print, and thermal transfer on paper
16" x 16"   1996

This is one in a series of works leading up to the final piece which was
commissioned by the Advanced Elastomer Systems L.P. for their 7th floor lobby.
The scene depicts the Ohio & Erie Canal as it was in 1827 featuring Lock 2, and
the J.W. Payne Boatyard. Also included is a subtle rendition of the 1996 Akron
Skyline as it appears from where this piece was hung in the AES Building.
Captain John Malvin, who played an important role in the canals history is
depicted in the background on his boat, while the artist is also shown as if walking
through the different scenes of past and present.

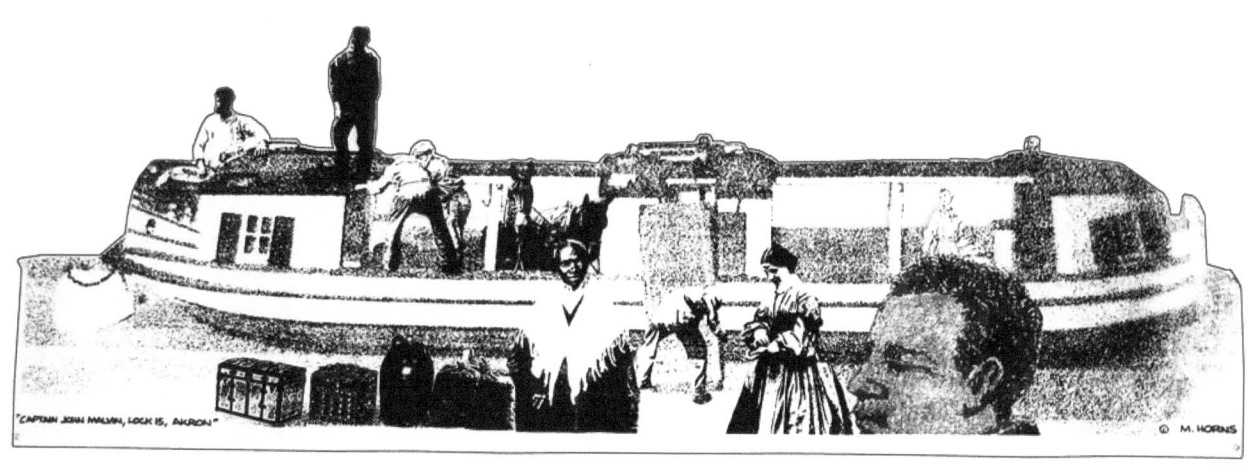

Captain John Malvin, Lock 15, Akron   electrostatic print on paper, laminated   21.25" x 61"   1995

This work depicts Malvin's packet, The Auburn, and the activity attendent to the packet's loading and unloading. Malvin was the only black man documented as owning his own canal boat in the United States in the 1840's He used a predominantly black crew. He also worked to integrate the First Baptist Church in Cleveland, organized a school for blacks, aiding the cause of the Underground Railroad, and wrote an autobiography, *North to Freedom*.
Malvin distinguished himself as a proud and dignified member of the community, a role model for all citizens.

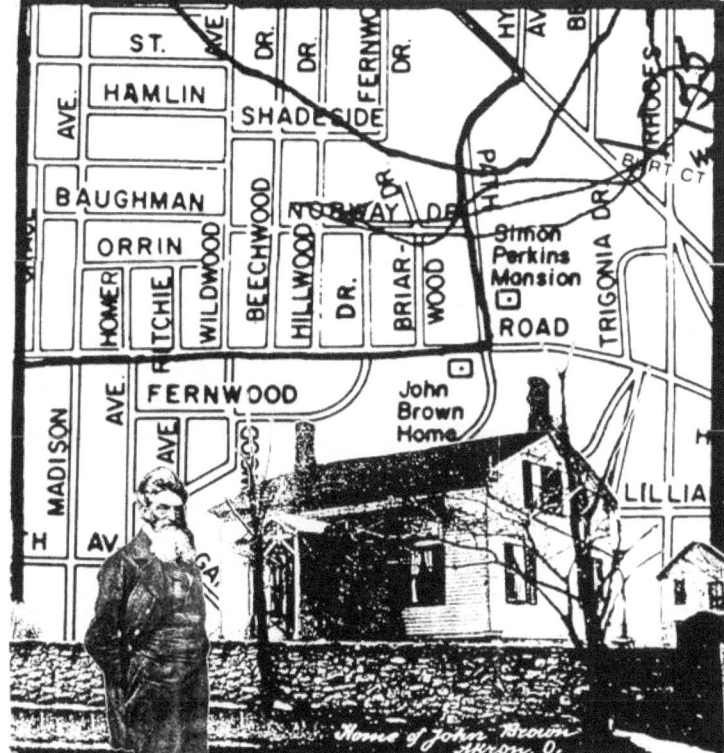

Home of John Brown, Akron Ohio
electrostatic print on paper, laminated 22" x 24"

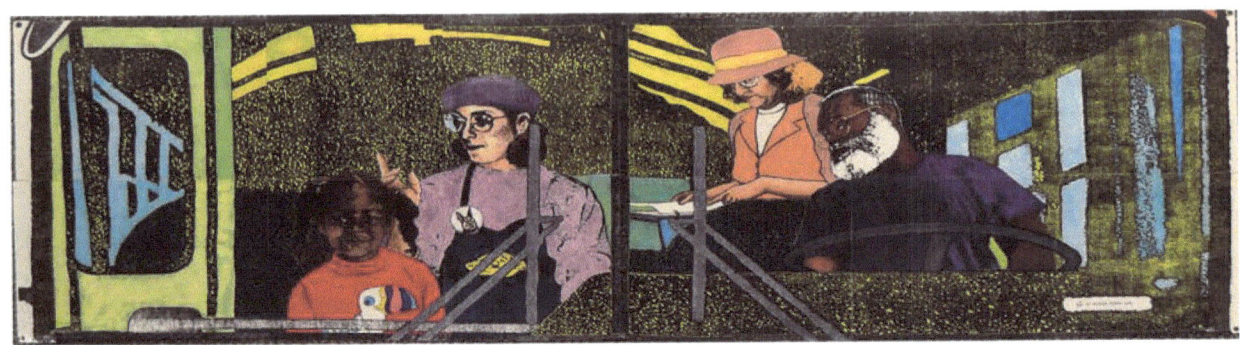

Field Trip   electrostatic print, thermal color transfer and mixed media on paper laminated   17" x 54.5"   1993

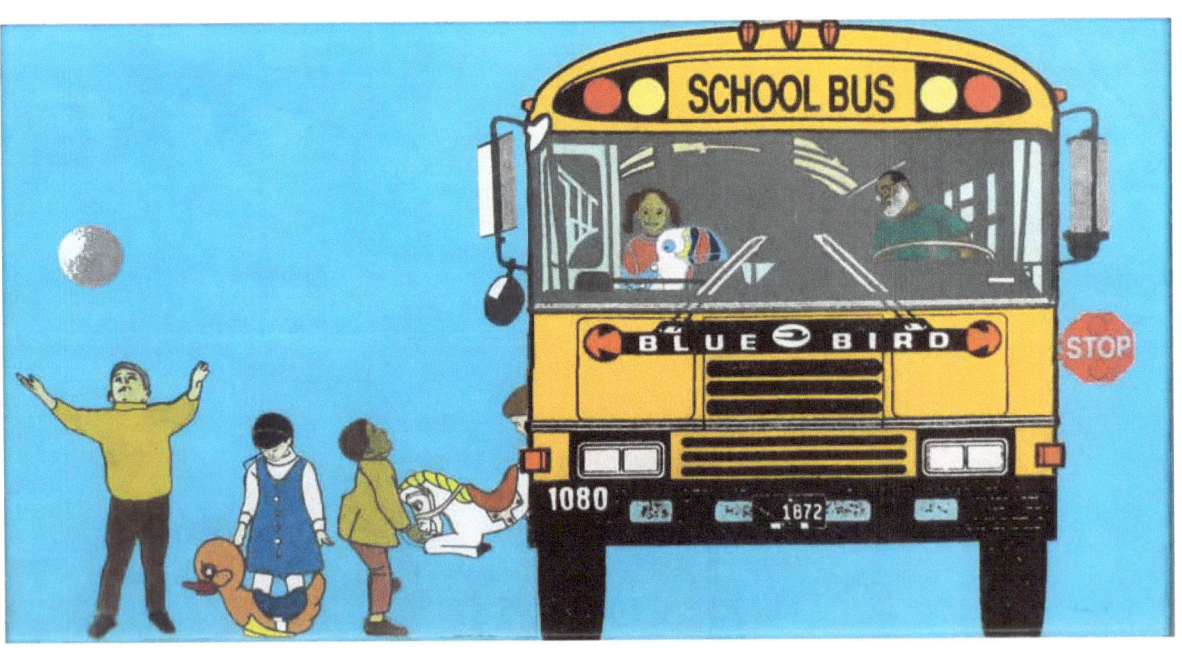

School Bus   electrostatic print, thermal color transfer on paper laminated 10" x 17"   1992

This was a version of a large commissioned piece for the Akron Children's Hospital

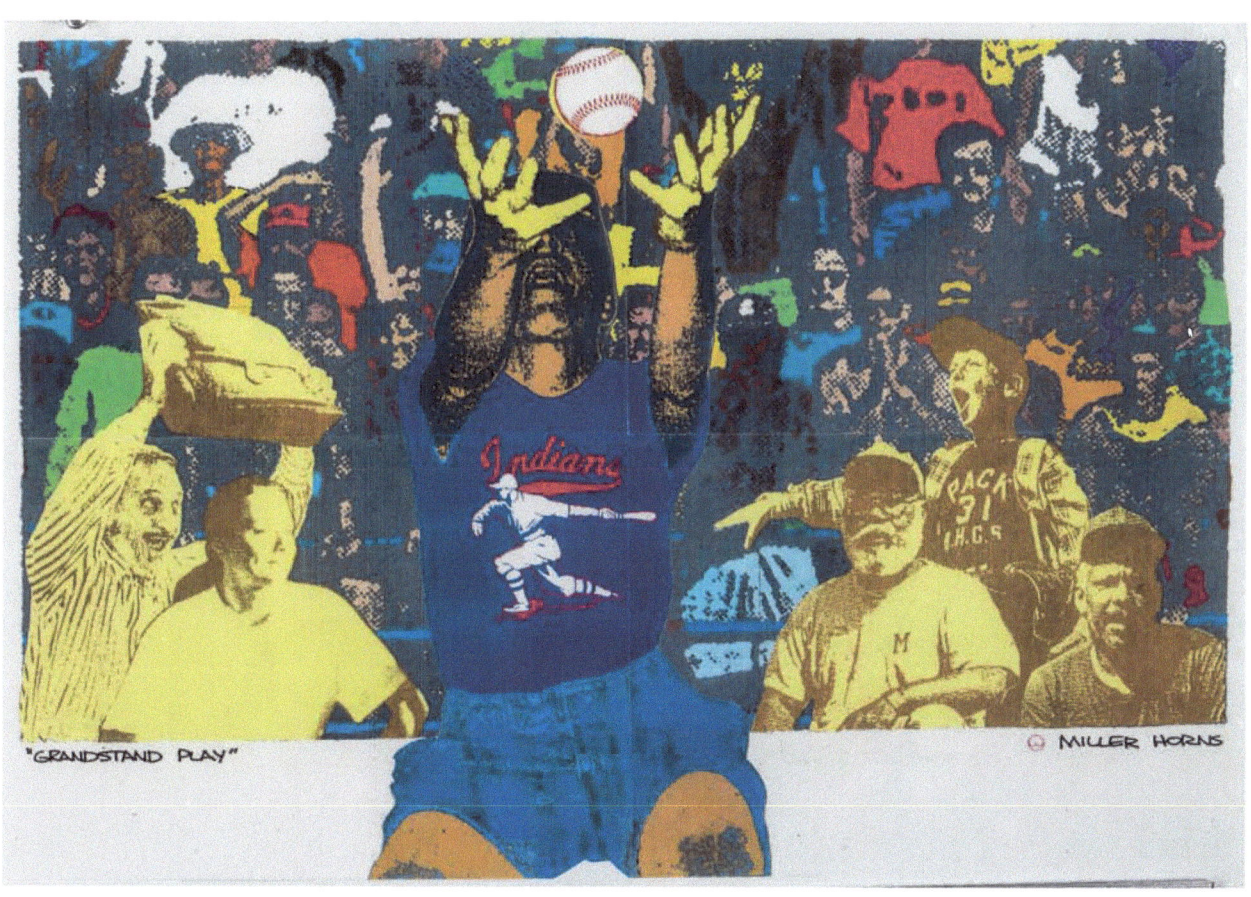

Grand Stand Play electrostatic print, thermal color transfer on paper
laminated 22" x 32"   circa 1997

This was a proposal for a commission work for the Jacob's Field Concourse.
It was not accepted and so never produced in a larger size. The
audience in the background is composed of Horns, his friends and
acquaintances. True to form, he almost always used live models for his works
that required people posing in some fashion. Even the young boy catching
the ball was posed and photographed by Miller.

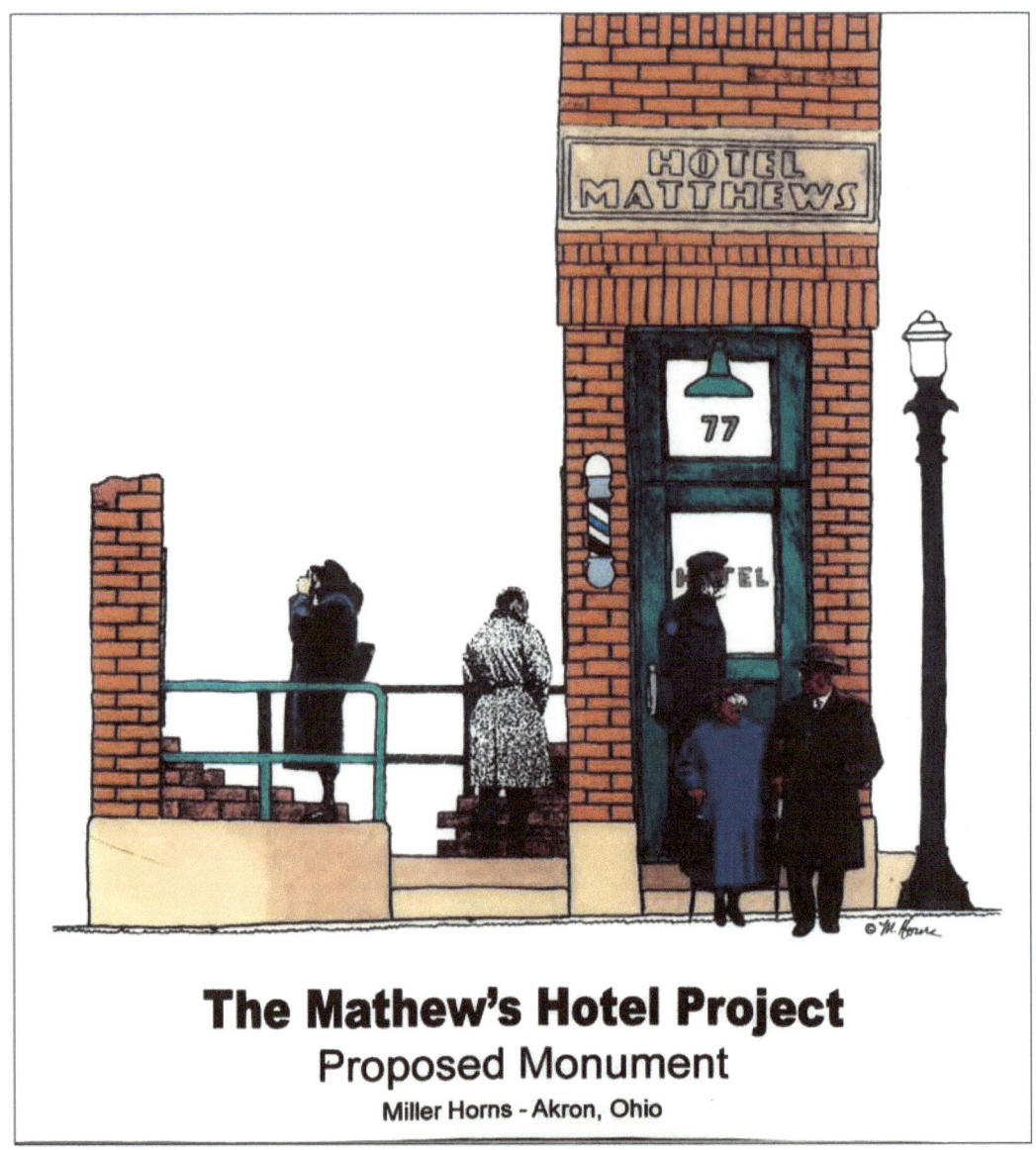

The Mathew's Hotel Project
Proposed Monument
Miller Horns - Akron, Ohio

A Monument to a Time and Place, The Mathews Hotel Project....one of many electrostatic prints depicting Horns vision for the Mathews Hotel Monument.

Horns proposal for this monument stated his idea to build a structure commemorating The Mathews Hotel: a cornerstone of African - American culture during the golden age of Howard St (Akron, Ohio). The structure was intended to replicate a portion of the old Mathews Hotel on or near its original location. It was to be 20' long, 15' high and 10' deep, and would have light and sound components. The structure would serve as the cornerstone of memory, recreating the feeling of a flourishing time past, while at the same time serving as a new foundation, the beginning of pride and accomplishment. He hoped the sculpture would instill memories of a proud African - American environment.

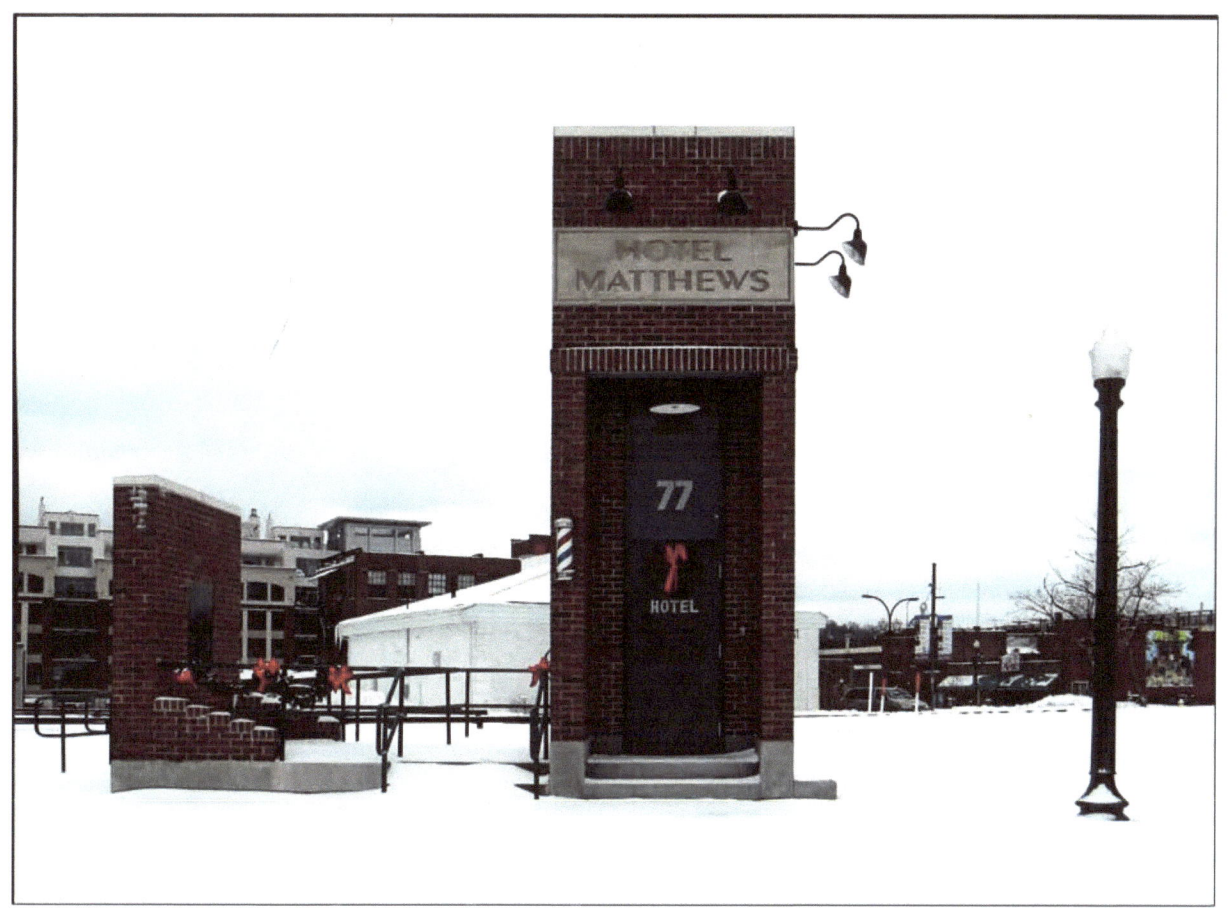

The finished monument   color photograph   8" x 10"   December 2013
photograph courtesy of Terry Klausman

The 1930 - 1950 era saw the heyday of Howard St, as a vibrant cultural center
of the African-American community in Akron Ohio. The Mathews Hotel was
built by entrepreneur George Mathews in 1925 and quickly became the anchor
of the Howard Street district. The Mathews was a regular stop for Black
entertainers such as Cab Calloway, Ella Fitzgerald, Louis Armstrong, and
Count Basie when they performed in Akron. The Mathews was the only hotel
these entertainers were allowed to stay in. Local music clubs included the
Green Turtle, The High Hat, the Cosmopolitan and Benny Rivers'. The Howard
Street district declined in the 1960's and much of it was razed for "urban
renewal" in the 1970's and 1980's. Horns considered the monument, his work
of art to be his gift to all of the people of the City of Akron.

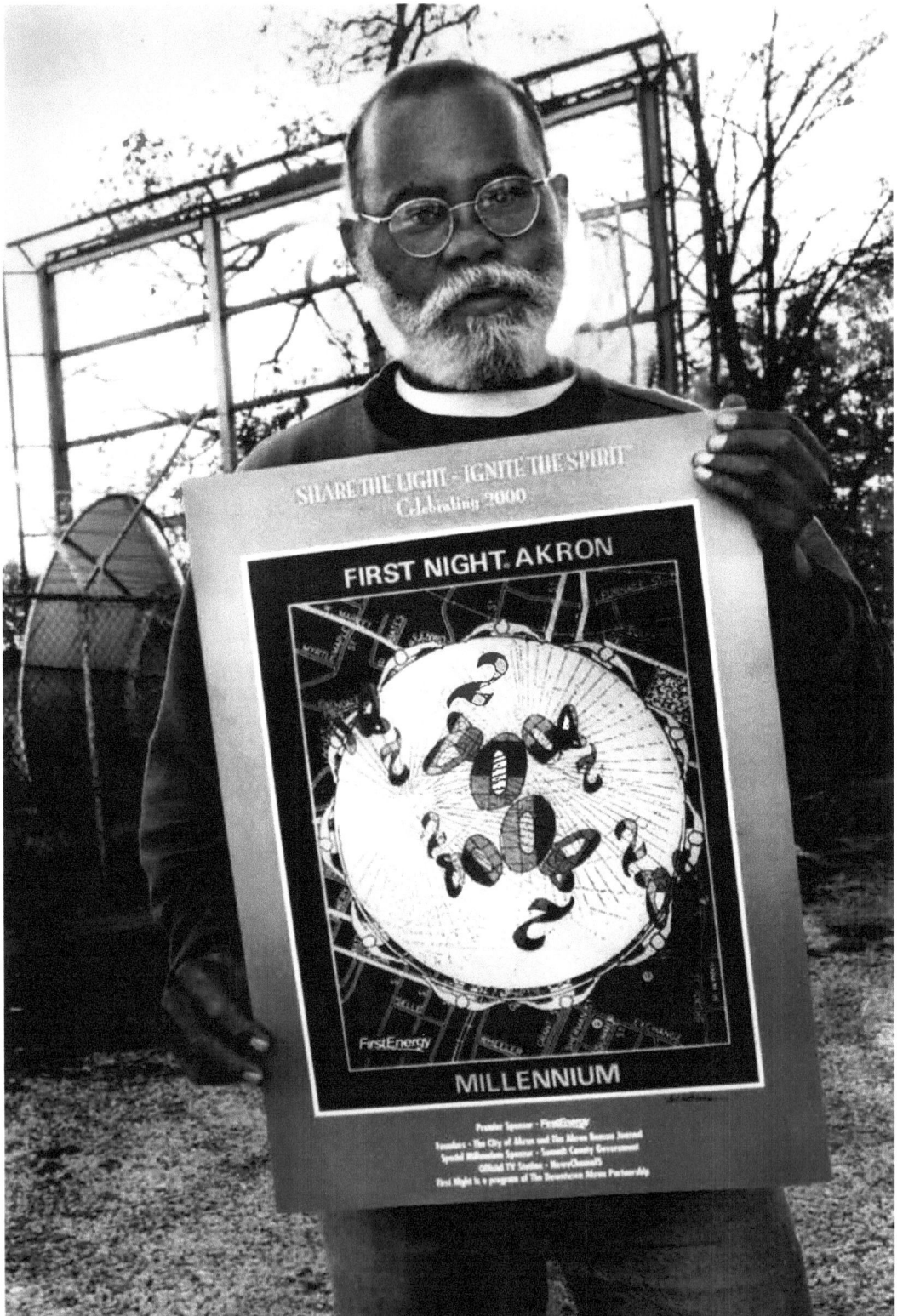

Maquette for Guitarmania (front side) commission
electrostatic print on paper, laminated
128" x 38"   2002

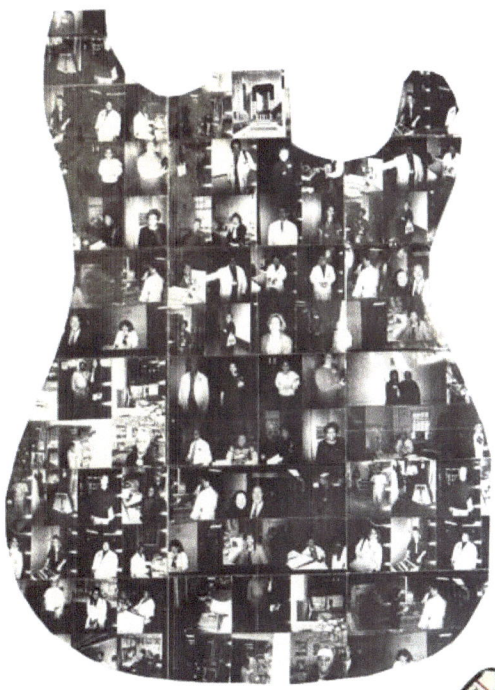

Detail for Guitarmania (back side)
electrostatic print on paper, laminated
128" x 38"   2002

The photos on the back side of Horns
guitar were taken during his hospitalization
for a heart attack, note the many
photos of nurses and doctors in lab coats.

Facing page:
photo of Miller Horns
holding his First Night Design Poster
2000
Horns was awarded the commission for
Akron's First Night button and poster
design in 1999. First Night is a city
wide New Year's Eve celebration that
takes place on the streets of Akron

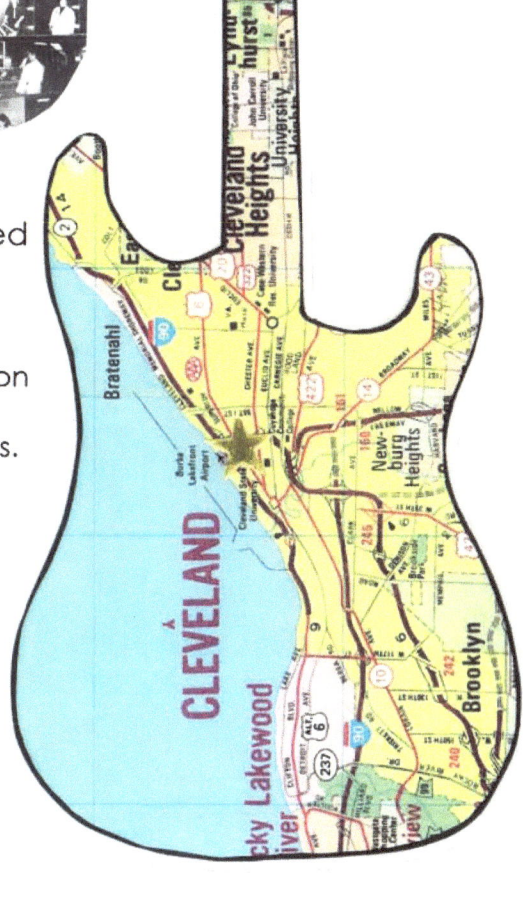

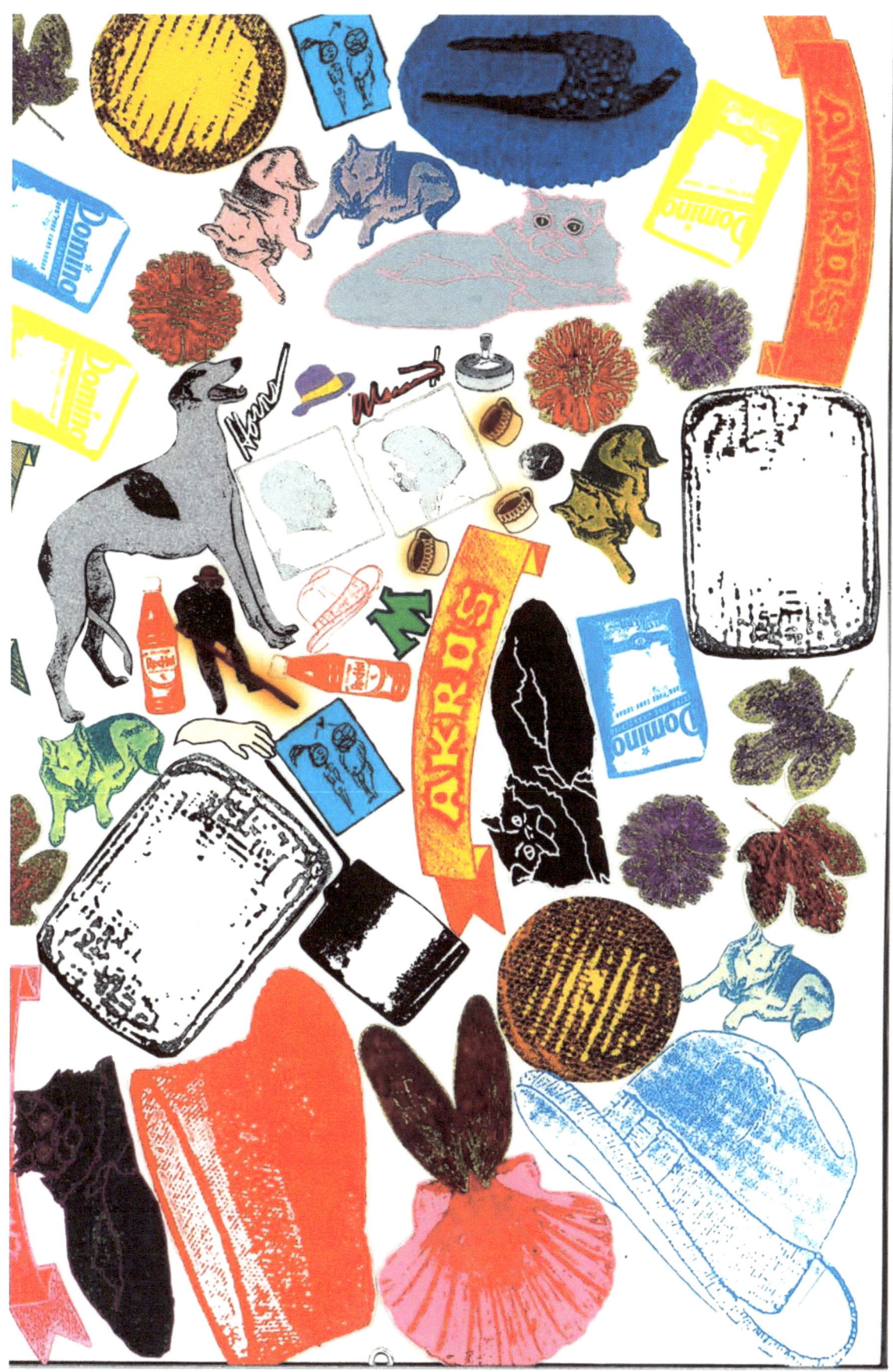